Primary
Language Arts
Grade 3

NSC Edition

Jennifer Peek
Heather Raymond
Mitzie-Ann Jackson

The Publishers would like to thank the following for permission to reproduce copyright material.

Text credits

p.29: 'Carnival' © Valerie Bloom 2007 from Celebrate! Poems about festivals around the world (Cambridge University Press) reprinted by permission of Eddison Pearson Ltd on behalf of Valerie Bloom; p.162: © World Health Organization; p.238 & 252: © 'First and Last' poem by Brian Moses from Reading Planet, Wriggle Room poetry collection; p.259: 'We are all different' poem by Judith Gorgone.

Photo credits

p.16: (tl) © Syda Productions/stock.adobe.com, (tr) © baibaz/stock.adobe.com, (c) © vitalyzorkin/stock.adobe.com, (cl) © Art_Photo/stock.adobe.com, (cr) © Rawpixel.com/stock.adobe.com, (bl) © diego cervo/stock.adobe.com, (br) © pololia/stock.adobe.com; p.27: © amnach/stock.adobe.com, © Africa Studio/stock.adobe.com, © lucky-photo/stock.adobe.com, © Dmitry Vereshchagin/stock.adobe.com, © dlyastokiv/stock.adobe.com, © Dusty Cline/stock.adobe.com, © Mike/stock.adobe.com, © Debbie Ann Powell/stock.adobe.com; p.29: (t) © BEEE/Shutterstock.com, (b) © Laiotz/Shutterstock.com; p.32: © nanettegrebe/stock.adobe.com; p.33: © Pete Niesen/Shutterstock; p.39: © twinsterphoto/stock.adobe.com; p.66: (tl) © pilipphoto/stock.adobe.com, (tr) © New Africa/stock.adobe.com, (cl) © Samuel B./stock.adobe.com, (cr) © Monkey Business/stock.adobe.com; p.68: (l) © didesign/stock.adobe.com, (c) © Anatoliy Karlyuk/stock.adobe.com, (r) © Sea Wave/stock.adobe.com; p.77: (l) © Satoshi Kina/stock.adobe.com, (c) © soupstock/stock.adobe.com, (r) © Rawpixel.com/stock.adobe.com; p.90: (l) © Alison Toon/stock.adobe.com, (c) © Solarisys/stock.adobe.com, (r) © FomaA/stock.adobe.com; p.152: © deagreez/stock.adobe.com; p.162: © michaeljung/stock.adobe.com; p.168: (tl) © Fractal Pictures/stock.adobe.com, (tc) © Ixepop/stock.adobe.com, (tr) © Gorodenkoff/Shutterstock, (bl) © Carlos David/stock.adobe.com, (br) © wavebreak3/stock.adobe.com; p.181: (tl) © Daniel Jędzura/stock.adobe.com, (tc) © Photo&Graphic Stock/stock.adobe.com, (tr) © PhotoSerg/stock.adobe.com, (bl) © Arcady/stock.adobe.com, (br) © Ashley van Dyck/stock.adobe.com; p.187: © Katerina_AR/Shutterstock; p.209: (tl) © Martin/stock.adobe.com, (tr) © Gan/stock.adobe.com, (bl) © PiyawatNandeenoparit/stock.adobe.com, (br) © jes2uphoto/stock.adobe.com; p.232: (t) © Tryfonov/stock.adobe.com, (c, b) © Argus/stock.adobe.com; p.241: © Narupon/stock.adobe.com, © trahko/stock.adobe.com, © New Africa/stock.adobe.com, © Rawpixel.com/stock.adobe.com, © leekris/stock.adobe.com; p.266: © Anneke/stock.adobe.com; p.273: (l) © amorn/stock.adobe.com, (c) © LIGHTFIELD STUDIOS/stock.adobe.com, (r) © blazekg/stock.adobe.com; p.277: © orenthomasphotography/Shutterstock; p.278: © DreanA/stock.adobe.com; p.282: (l) © Monkey Business/stock.adobe.com, (cl) © micromonkey/stock.adobe.com, (cr) © mezzotint_fotolia/stock.adobe.com, (r) © MandriaPix/stock.adobe.com; p.307: © WavebreakMediaMicro/stock.adobe.com; p.316: (t) © luismolinero/stock.adobe.com, (b) © Frank Wagner/stock.adobe.com; p.320: (tl) © bergamont/stock.adobe.com, (tr) © kovaleva_ka/stock.adobe.com, (bl) © shaitan1985/stock.adobe.com, (br) © Li Ding/stock.adobe.com.

Hachette UK's policy is to use papers that are natural, renewable and recyclable products and made from wood grown in well-managed forests and other controlled sources. The logging and manufacturing processes are expected to conform to the environmental regulations of the country of origin.

To order, please visit www.hoddereducation.com or contact Customer Service at education@hachette.co.uk / +44 (0)1235 827827.

ISBN: 9781398352919

© Jennifer Peek, Heather Raymond, Mitzie-Ann Jackson and Hodder & Stoughton Limited 2024

This edition published in 2024 by

Hodder Education,

An Hachette UK Company

Carmelite House

50 Victoria Embankment

London EC4Y 0DZ

www.hoddereducation.com

Impression number 10 9 8 7 6 5 4 3 2 1

Year 2027 2026 2025 2024

All rights reserved. Apart from any use permitted under UK copyright law, no part of this publication may be reproduced or transmitted in any form or by any means, electronic or mechanical, including photocopying and recording, or held within any information storage and retrieval system, without permission in writing from the publisher or under licence from the Copyright Licensing Agency Limited. Further details of such licences (for reprographic reproduction) may be obtained from the Copyright Licensing Agency Limited, www.cla.co.uk

Cover illustration by Heather Clarke c/o D'Avila Illustration Agency

Illustrations by Heather Clarke c/o D'Avila Illustration Agency and Hyphen S.A.

Typeset by Hyphen S.A.

Printed in Spain

A catalogue record for this title is available from the British Library.

Contents

Contents...3

Term 1 **Unit 1**

Chapter 1 10

Speaking and listening: Play a whispering game.. 10

Word builder: Recognise long vowel sounds in words; identify whether vowel sound is at beginning or middle of word; write a sentence including long vowel sound words.......................... 12

Let's read: Interpret pictures and answer questions; differentiate between beginning, middle and end of story; use a graphic organiser to sequence a story; retell a story in your own words; identify the moral of the story 14

Grammar builder: Plural endings; inflectional endings; regular and irregular nouns 16

Let's write: Read a story and create a story plan for it; use the story plan to tell the story in your own words 18

Chapter 2 20

Speaking and listening: Study a picture, discuss and answer questions; discuss rules as a group and make notes; feed back to whole class 20

Word builder: Identify words within words; complete sentences with missing word................ 22

Let's read: Read an advertisement for a school; look up/discuss the meanings of any unknown words; compare the advertisement with own school; make notes; complete comparative table 24

Grammar builder: Use conjunctions to link parts of sentences; complete sentences with missing words and conjunctions.. 26

Let's write: Write down your school rules; write two additional rules of your own.......................... 28

Chapter 3 29

Speaking and listening: Read a poem aloud; identify Jamaican Creole words and compare with Standard Jamaican English; identify verbs in sentences; retell the events in the poem in sequence; plan and present a performance of the poem in groups... 29

Word builder: Use adjectives to describe personal response to poem; descriptive writing; identify and use proper nouns correctly............. 31

Let's read: Read a non-fiction text about the Jamaican flag; use description, colour in the flag; identify adjectives and nouns in the text; answer *true* or *false* questions; relate to own experience.. 33

Grammar builder: More work on identifying and using adjectives 35

Let's write: Plan and write a descriptive paragraph; use a graphic organiser to make notes; write complete sentences........................... 37

Chapter 4 39

Speaking and listening: Learn vocabulary describing the body; group discussion 39

Word builder: Complete words with missing vowels; learn sounds *pl*, *ck* and *ss* 41

Let's read: Prepositions; read a non-fiction text and answer questions 43

Grammar builder: Comparative adjectives; use correct form/spelling of comparative adjectives and superlatives; inflectional endings 45

Let's write: Plan and write a short presentation on parts of the body; use prompts to structure presentation... 48

Chapter 5 50

Speaking and listening: Read and listen to haiku; write a haiku poem and read it to your partner 50

Word builder: Vocabulary about healthy eating; practise spelling; syllabification; alphabetical order; add missing words to complete sentences; relate to own experience and write about it...... 52

Let's read: Read a non-fiction text on healthy foodstuffs, and answer questions; relate to own experience and express a view 54

Grammar builder: Introduce demonstratives "this", "that", "these", "those"; add correct demonstrative to complete sentences; write sentences using demonstrativess........................... 56

Let's write: Complete a food diary for a day; record answers to questions about the diary; in pairs or groups plan and write a well-balanced menu 58

Chapter 6 60

Speaking and listening: Review, discuss and evaluate the experience of making a presentation (Chapter 4); review and discuss the experience of listening to presentations 60

Word builder: Read words aloud and mime their meaning; complete sentences by adding missing word; sort words into nouns, verbs and adjectives; identify *fl, gr* and *pr* sounds in words 62

Let's read: Read a non-fiction text and answer comprehension questions; compile a list of suitable adjectives 64

Grammar builder: Use the word "not" to write statements and opposites; prepositions 66

Let's write: Prepare and write a short presentation on a theme of looking after your body; use prompts to plan the presentation; write and deliver the presentation 68

Term 1 Unit 1 Review and assessment 70

Term 1   Unit 2

Chapter 7 73

Speaking and listening: Discuss and make notes of news from different members of the class; draw and label a picture of one item of news and present it to the class 73

Word builder: Vocabulary relating to news; choose words to complete sentences; identify number of syllables in words; identify words within words 75

Let's read: Pre-reading activities discussing different types of news report; derive information from photographs; summarise and evaluate information; describe pictures using nouns, adjectives and verbs; study pictures and written reports, match correct picture to written report 77

Grammar builder: Identify nouns and adjectives in news reports; re-write sentences using adjectives 79

Let's write: Use a picture cue, write a news report; use a writing frame to structure a report; review and expand the report 81

Chapter 8 84

Speaking and listening: Talk about an item you own which is special to you; make notes to refer to while giving a talk; ask and answer questions 84

Word builder: Read words aloud; use a dictionary or online reference; choose words to complete sentences; write descriptive sentences; identify words with "pl", "bl", "fl", "pr", "br" or "cr" consonant blends 86

Let's read: Read a simple story; describe characters in the story; discuss the story and share responses 88

Grammar builder: Select adjectives to describe pictures; write descriptive sentences and identify adjectives 90

Let's write: Write descriptive sentences; read a description of an object and draw it from the description 92

Chapter 9 94

Speaking and listening: Read a paragraph and identify key points for a summary; talk to a partner and make notes to summarise what they tell you 94

Word builder: Read key sight words aloud to familiarise them; select words to complete sentences; spell words from memory 96

Let's read: Take turns to read a story aloud; number pictures in correct order; write headings for the story sections; predict what happens next 98

Grammar builder: Learn about verbs and tenses; past tense; regular and irregular verb endings; complete past tense sentences by adding verbs 100

Let's write: Write an account in the past tense about a special event; use a planner to make notes; write and check your story 102

Chapter 10 104

Speaking and listening: Match headlines to pictures; write a headline and draw a picture to accompany a news story; talk to a partner about your news story; listen to your partner's news story; ask and answer questionss 104

Contents

Word builder: Read words aloud in style of news reader; select words to complete sentences; write a short news story based on a given headline; identify *sk*, *dr*, *fr*, *gr*, *st* and *sl* sounds in words; use a spelling pyramid to spell more difficult words.. 106

Let's read: Read a newspaper article and answer comprehension questions; use a dictionary; write definitions of words 108

Grammar builder: Adverbs; use adverbs in sentences; write sentences using adverbs..........110

Let's write: Write a news article about an event; take turns to act as reporter and witness; conduct interviews; plan and write a report 112

Chapter 11 114

Speaking and listening: Listen to a story; follow a story by looking at pictures; use strategies to understand words; re-tell a story in the correct sequence; identify four key parts of the story 114

Word builder: Read words aloud and count syllables; identify *i* and *e* sounds of letter "y"; list words according to number of syllables; identify vocabulary words in a text; use vocabulary words in own writing; add missing letters to complete words correctly 116

Let's read: Read a title, discuss and predict; read a story; predict what characters in the story will do next; identify adverbs in the story..................118

Grammar builder: Use pronouns; subject verb agreement; identify mistakes in sentences and re-write correctly; complete sentences by adding missing verb 120

Let's write: Write a short story in the past tense; use a graphic organiser to plan writing; discuss story with partner; write story 123

Chapter 12 125

Speaking and listening: Take turns to read and follow instructions 125

Word builder: Vocabulary related to making things; read words aloud; identify missing word; use vocabulary words to complete sentences to make meaningful instructions; long vowel sound in r-controlled vowels..................................126

Let's read: Read instructions for a computer game; describe and draw an avatar................... 128

Grammar builder: Identify pronouns, adjectives and adverbs in text; write a description using pronouns, adjectives and adverbs; write sentences in the past tense 130

Let's write: Design a poster to promote a computer game; identify key facts to include 132

Term 1 Unit 2 Review and assessment 133

Term 2 Unit 1

Chapter 13 137

Speaking and listening: Read a speech aloud; plan and draft a speech using a graphic organiser and role play the speech...137

Word builder: Read words aloud, identifying the *ar* sound; use words containing "ar" to complete sentences; write your own sentences including "ar" words; use antonyms in sentences 139

Let's read: Read a text about community; express a view; answer comprehension questions; make a list; write a descriptive sentence............141

Grammar builder: Use full stops and commas; add punctuation to sentences; insert correct adverb in sentences 143

Let's write: Plan and write a paragraph about your community; write a first draft following a sequence plan; read and edit each other's drafts; write a final draft 145

Chapter 14 147

Speaking and listening: Working in pairs, students take turns to describe a picture and to draw what is described 147

Word builder: Read selection of words aloud and identify the same sound in each; add words to complete sentences; write sentences using vocabulary words; use vocabulary words to describe a picture; write synonyms..................... 149

Let's read: Look at a picture and answer pre-reading questions; write synonyms; read a news report; complete missing words and phrases; make a summary 151

Grammar builder: Subject verb agreement; use pronouns; identify the verb and the subject n sentences; verb forms in the past tense........ 154

5

Let's write: Plan and write notes for a speech agreeing or disagreeing with a statement; work in a team to share tasks; structure a speech in sections; deliver a speech; ask and answer questions 157

Chapter 15 159

Speaking and listening: Look at a picture and discuss with a partner; identify and discuss dangers; agree, write and read aloud safety rules 159

Word builder: Vocabulary about safety in the home; identify diphthongs in words; use vocabulary words to complete sentences; divide vocabulary words into syllables 160

Let's read: Read a non-fiction text and answer comprehension questions; draw a picture and write a caption 162

Grammar builder: Past simple tense; regular and irregular verb endings; add correct form of past simple verb to complete sentences; write the past simple form of verbs; differentiate between final sound *id*, *d* or *t* 164

Let's write: Use topic, supporting and concluding sentences in structuring a paragraph; write a report consisting of two paragraphs using sentence prompts; read and comment on each other's reports before writing a final version 166

Chapter 16 168

Speaking and listening: Use pictures to talk about different jobs; discuss in small groups, sharing experiences and opinions; make notes of discussion and give a short speech 168

Word builder: Vocabulary around community safety; identify number of syllables in words; use vocabulary words to complete haiku; group synonyms under correct heading 170

Let's read: Read a radio interview script and answer comprehension questions, citing evidence in text 172

Grammar builder: Plural and singular common and proper nouns; differentiate between masculine, feminine and gender neutral/neuter nouns; apostrophe of possession 174

Let's write: Write an interview dialogue including questions and answers 176

Chapter 17 177

Speaking and listening: Discuss road safety rules and identify an action for each command; draw something to symbolise each command; discuss and write notes about road safety rules 177

Word builder: Vocabulary about staying safe; read words aloud and identify *ur/or* sound; select correct word to complete sentences; homonyms, homophones and homographs; complete sentences using correct homophone; use a dictionary to find different meanings for homographs; find homophones and write meanings 179

Let's read: Read a non-fiction text and answer comprehension questions; identify signs and say where you would see them; write a sentence explaining what each sign means; discuss warning signs and write notes 181

Grammar builder: Use possessive apostrophe with single noun; make direction signs 183

Let's write: Make notes about dangerous places; plan, design and label a warning sign; write a draft of a paragraph using topic, supporting and concluding sentences; check and write a neat draft 185

Chapter 18 187

Speaking and listening: Listen to a report about the weather and answer comprehension questions; take turns to read and discuss the report; share your thoughts with the class 187

Word builder: Vocabulary about aspects of safety; read aloud; use a dictionary; complete newspaper headlines with missing word; prefixes, root words and suffixes 189

Let's read: Look at a picture and answer questions; read a non-fiction text and answer questions; in groups discuss questions about the subject 191

Grammar builder: Past participles; differentiate between present simple tense, past simple tense and past participle in regular and irregular verbs 193

Let's write: Rewrite a news story in your own words, using "when, who, where, what" structure; write a paragraph using topic, supporting and concluding sentences 195

Term 2 Unit 1 Review and assessment 196

Contents

Term 2 **Unit 2**

Chapter 19 .... **199**

Speaking and listening: Listen to a biographical text and answer *true* or *false* questions; read text aloud, underlining key words/phrases; summarise text.. 199

Word builder: Vocabulary about jobs; read words aloud in different tones of voice; identify "er" and "or" word endings.. 201

Let's read: Read about poetic devices; write sentences using alliteration; identify rhyming words; read a tongue twister............................... 203

Grammar builder: Use apostrophe of possession; differentiate between plural *s* and possessive *s* 205

Let's write: Write an informal letter using a template 207

Chapter 20 .... **209**

Speaking and listening: Look at pictures, discuss and answer questions; using a map, discuss crops which are grown in Jamaica..................................... 209

Word builder: Vocabulary about farming and agriculture; divide words into syllables; select words to complete sentences; identify and define homonyms 211

Let's read: Read a bar graph and answer questions; research and write a report using an outline template 213

Grammar builder: Comparative and superlative adjectives with regular and irregular forms; complete sentences using the correct form of adjective; write the key information about comparative and superlative adjectivess......... 215

Let's write: Choose one Jamaican crop to research; complete a mind map; draft and deliver a presentation 217

Chapter 21 .... **219**

Speaking and listening: Read advertisements aloud; differentiate between different advertisements; discuss who would find the advertisements appealing 219

Word builder: Vocabulary about advertising; use vocabulary in context; use a dictionary; identify *oy* and *oi* sound in words; use "oy" and "oi" words in sentences.. 221

Let's read: Read advertisements and answer questions; select an advertisement and discuss/explain your choice 223

Grammar builder: Use conjunctions "when", "where", "while", "but" 224

Let's write: Write an advertisement for a new invention; write a name for the invention; plan the advertisement using a mind map 226

Chapter 22 .... **228**

Speaking and listening: Discuss with a partner your food, clothes and objects around you; talk about importing and exporting; differentiate objects made in Jamaica... 228

Word builder: Vocabulary about buying and selling; unscramble letters to spell words; use mnemonics to reinforce spelling............................. 230

Let's read: Read a non-fiction text about the Caribbean and answer comprehension questions including deduction 232

Grammar builder: Use question words "who", "what", "why", "when", "where"; read a short text and answer questions 234

Let's write: Write an informal letter using letter template and prompt sentences 236

Chapter 23 .... **238**

Speaking and listening: Pre-speaking activity; read a poem aloud; identify alliteration and rhyming; discuss the message/meaning of the poem and share ideas and opinions 238

Word builder: Vocabulary relating to feelings; write sentences using vocabulary words; select correct comparative/superlative form to complete sentences 240

Let's read: Read a poem and explore an imaginative response; make an interpretation of the poem in a drawing; talk about the message of the poem; identify antonyms.......................... 242

Grammar builder: Punctuate questions; apostrophes of contraction; identify words with contractions; write out the full form of the words.. 244

Let's write: Write a poem following an outline structure; choose a theme; brainstorm vocabulary; write drafts; check spelling and punctuation.. 246

Chapter 24 248

Speaking and listening: Think about listening, play a listening game; ask and answer questions; talk descriptively.................................. 248

Word builder: Vocabulary relating to poetry, games and songs; use vocabulary words to complete sentences; devise mnemonics; complete sentences using synonyms and antonyms 250

Let's read: Read a poem; identify verse structure; identify rhyming words; express a personal response to the poem, relating to own experience.. 252

Grammar builder: Change positive sentences to negative sentences using full form of words and contracted words 254

Let's write: Write an acrostic poem about food 256

Term 2 Unit 2 Review and assessment 258

Term 3 Unit 1

Chapter 25 262

Speaking and listening: Sing rhymes and perform actions; discuss difference between living and non-living things...................... 262

Word builder: Vocabulary relating to living and non-living things; differentiate between words describing living and non-living things; write a simple four-line rhyme; use a dictionary........... 264

Let's read: Differentiate between fiction and non-fiction; read a non-fiction text including heading, sub-heading, picture, picture caption, table, bold type, and bar graph; answer comprehension questions; answer questions about the presentation of the text.................... 266

Grammar builder: Identify statements, exclamations and questions; use correct punctuation in statements, exclamations and questions; differentiate fiction and non-fiction texts in past and present tense............................ 269

Let's write: Write a non-fiction text; write two paragraphs on a chosen topic; research the topic; make notes and use graphic organiser; write drafts, check and re-write; include a photograph and caption, and a table or bar graph 271

Chapter 26 273

Speaking and listening: Talk about games you play and explain the rules; ask and answer questions; draw and label a picture showing a game.. 273

Word builder: Vocabulary about games and sports; write complete sentences using vocabulary words; use a dictionary; understand words can have different meanings; write sentences showing the different meanings of words... 275

Let's read: Skim a text for information; read a non-fiction text; express and explain a point of view; answer comprehension questions; match words; self-evaluate reading skills 277

Grammar builder: Re-write present tense text in past tense; identify verbs and change tense... 280

Let's write: Read a book about a sport or sportsperson and write a book report 282

Chapter 27 283

Speaking and listening: Listen to short texts and answer *true* or *false* questions; take turns to read texts aloud; discuss questions, share ideas with class.. 283

Word builder: Vocabulary related to folktales; identify syllables in words; identify synonyms; sound out words with silent letters; add missing silent letters to complete words 285

Let's read: List adjectives to describe fictional characters; read a folktale and retell the story in your own words; discuss the moral of the story 287

Grammar builder: Identify verbs in a text; re-write verbs from past tense to future; complete sentences with correct verb form 289

Let's write: Work in a group to tell stories; plan and write a summary of your story including characters, beginning, middle, end and moral; read and discuss summaries in groups; discuss moral of stories and what can be learned from them.. 291

Chapter 28 293

Speaking and listening: Talk about proverbs in Jamaican Creole and Standard Jamaican English; research and write out proverbs; discuss the meanings of different proverbs; ask and answer questions.. 293

Word builder: Vocabulary related to sayings and proverbs; count syllables; use a dictionary; complete sentences with vocabulary words; inflectional ending "-ing" 295

Let's read: Read information text on proverbs and answer comprehension questions 297

Grammar builder: Use speech marks; roleplay a telephone conversation; use exclamation marks; write a telephone dialogue with correct punctuation 299

Let's write: Read a story and write a continuation of the story, using dialogue 301

Chapter 29 303

Speaking and listening: Discuss the different languages spoken in the Caribbean; identify proper nouns; work in groups to research another country in the Caribbean and present your results; ask and answer questions; choose which country you would like to live in and explain why 303

Word builder: Vocabulary about the Caribbean region; complete sentences with missing word; using context clues to understand unfamiliar words 305

Let's read: Differentiate between fact and opinion; self-evaluate reading skills; differentiate between fiction and non-fiction 307

Grammar builder: Use full stops, question marks and exclamation marks; use the conjunction "but" 309

Let's write: Read a book and write a book report 311

Chapter 30 312

Speaking and listening: Describe activities around you in the present continuous tense; look at a picture and describe it in the present continuous tense; think about what the picture might look like in the future and discuss your ideas 312

Word builder: Words containing the letter "x"; sound the words to hear the different sound which "x" makes; sound words and identify a silent letter 314

Let's read: Read an article and answer questions; express and justify an opinion 316

Grammar builder: Use apostrophes of possession; use the future tense 318

Let's write: Differentiate positive and negative sentences; complete sentences with correct form of contracted words and apostrophe of contraction 320

Term 3 Unit 1 Review and assessment 322

TERM 1

Unit 1

This term will include learning about classroom rules, the Jamaican flag, our body and eating healthy food, as well as other interesting topics.

Chapter 1

Speaking and listening

1. Play *The Secret Counting Game*. You can play this game in your seat, or you can sit or stand in a circle.

   Instructions

   - Choose a student to start the game. This student thinks of a number between 10 and 30 and only lets the teacher know their number.

- The teacher says "Start!". The first student whispers their number quietly to the person on their left. For example, "twelve".
- The student on the left then whispers the next number to the person on their left. For example, "thirteen".
- The student on the left then whispers "fourteen" and so on.
- Do this until you have gone all the way around the circle.
- When the whisper reaches the last student, they say their number out loud for everyone to hear.
- Is it the correct number? Check with your teacher if you are not sure.

Extra challenge

For an extra challenge, try starting with a number between 40 and 60 and count backwards.

Remember ☆☆☆

A **whisper** is very soft and quiet.
Stay still and silent or you may not hear it.

Term 1 Unit 1

Word builder

Look and learn

In some words, the vowels *a, e, i, o, u* are **long**. Often, this is because two vowels work together. For example, in the word "**a**p**e**", the *a* and *e* make a long vowel sound. In the word "s**ai**l", the vowels *a* and *i* work together to make a long sound.

1 Match the pictures with the words.

Word box

apron	sail	aim	ape
nail	ate	mail	pain
age	rain		

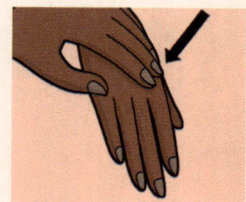    

2 Work with your partner. Take turns to say the words aloud.

3 Circle the correct answer:
  1 For the top row of pictures, the *a* sound is pronounced <u>at the beginning</u> / <u>in the middle</u> of the word.
  2 For the bottom row of pictures, the *a* sound is pronounced <u>at the beginning</u> / <u>in the middle</u> of the word.

4 Select a word from the top row of pictures in Activity 1 and write a sentence including that word. Do the same for the bottom row. Then compare your sentences with a partner.

> Example:
> The apes are eating bananas.

1 _____

2 _____

Term 1 Unit 1

Let's read

Look at these pictures. They tell the story about what happened one day in Mrs Walker's class.

Marcus at 10 a.m.   Marcus at 6 p.m.

1 In pairs, read the questions and possible answers about what is happening in picture 1.

Beginning (picture 1)

What is the setting in this picture? It is a school classroom.

- What is happening in the picture? The teacher is speaking but Marcus is not listening.
- How do you know that Marcus is not listening? He is thinking about playing football.

2 In pairs, read the questions and complete the answers for picture 2.

Middle (picture 2)

1 Where is Marcus? Explain how you know.

_____

_____

2 Is he finding the homework easy or difficult? Why?

_____

_____

14

Chapter 1

3 In pairs, complete the answers for your own conclusion to this story.

End (your own conclusion)

- What happened next?
  _____

- How did the story end?
  _____

4 Look at the graphic organiser below which is divided into three parts: the beginning, the middle and the end. Complete the organiser using short notes about the story. Use the questions and answers in Activity 1 to help you.

Beginning	Middle	End
Students learning / Teacher teaching / Boy not...		

5 Use your notes to tell the story to another pair of students in your own words.

6 Report back to the class and say what you think you can learn from this story.

L👀k and learn
An important lesson or a message that a story tells you is called the **moral of the story**.

Grammar builder

1 Read these two incorrect sentences. What is missing from the words *pencil* and *sandwich*?

Alison has five pencil.

Mark has two sandwich.

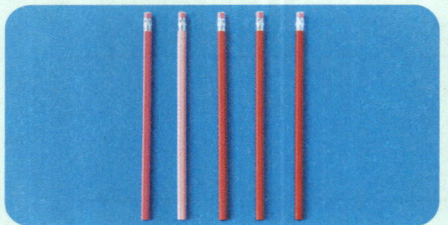

- Many nouns, like *pencil*, only need one extra letter **-s** to be added to the end. Other nouns like *sandwich* need **-es** to be added to the end. Nouns that do this are called **regular nouns**.

One pencil   Five pencil**s**

- Nouns that behave differently to this are called **irregular nouns**.
  Some nouns that end in **-y**, like *baby*, are irregular.
  The last letter is removed and three letters **-ies** are added to make the new ending.

One baby 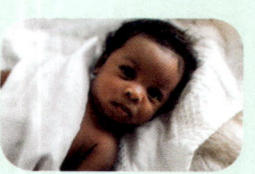   Two bab**ies**

Be careful! If there is a vowel before the **-y**, then you just add **-s**.

One boy    Two boy**s**

> **Remember** ☆☆☆
> Vowels are the letters **a**, **e**, **i**, **o** and **u**.

> **L👀k and learn**
> When you change the ending of a word and add a new ending, the new ending is called an **inflectional ending**. Inflectional endings create another form of the same word. In this case, the nouns become plural when you add the new ending.

2 What is the plural of each of these nouns? Check the rules if you are not sure.

city _____   cherry _____

boy _____   party _____

lady _____   key _____

tray _____   baby _____

family _____   birthday _____

3 Complete each sentence with a plural noun from Activity 2.

1 In Mrs Green's class, there are 12 girls and 15 _____.

2 A hospital is where _____ are born.

3 The waiters carried the food on _____.

4 Amy was invited to two _____ on the same day.

Let's write

1 Prepare to plan and write a story. Read the story below.

Mr Smith lives near a beautiful bay. One day, he was in the garden picking cherries from a bush when his dog Jack started to bark. Mr Smith went to see what the noise was about and he found Jack running around the garden playing with some keys. Jack was just about to bury the keys when Mr Smith got hold of his leash. "Silly dog!" said Mr Smith to Jack as he walked him back to the garden. Mr Smith had already picked a big bag of cherries and had to make jam from them before his boys came home from school in the city, on the bus. He put the cherries on a tray and carried them to the kitchen. He loved to make food for his family. That night, they were having a party to celebrate Mrs Smith's birthday. Mr Smith says Mrs Smith is the most beautiful lady he has ever seen.

2 If you had to plan this story before writing it, what would the plan look like? Complete the story plan on next page. Use short notes to write about the people, places and what happens in the story.

3 Without looking at the reading text, use your story plan to write the complete story in your notebook.

Chapter 1

Story Plan

Genre:

Characters:

Setting:

Plot:

Complication:

Resolution:

Useful words:

4 Read the completed story to your partner and explain how your story fits with your plan.

Remember ☆☆☆

Make sure that your sentences are punctuated. Check for full stops and capital letters.

Chapter 2

Speaking and listening

Can you imagine what a school with no rules might be like? Look at this picture closely.

1. With your partner, or in a small group, read and discuss these questions together:

   What has gone wrong here?

   What rules have been broken?

   How do you think the children in this class feel?

   Do all of the children feel the same way?

   Do you think this is a good classroom to be part of, or a bad classroom to be part of? Can you give some reasons why?

2. Look at the following rules for listening to and speaking with others. In small groups, discuss why these rules are important.

Example:
It is important to listen to the teacher so you can follow instructions.

- Listen to the teacher.
- Listen to others.
- Put your hand up if you want to speak.
- Keep hands / feet to yourselves.
- Respect each other.
- Respect other people's property.
- Take care of the classroom furniture.
- Bring the right stationery (pencils, books, …) to class.
- Use kind words.
- Concentrate on your learning.

Use this space to make some notes during your discussion:

3 After your discussion, be ready to share feedback with the class about your answers.

Term 1 Unit 1

Word builder

L👀k and learn

One way you can work out word meanings is to look for words within words. Look at the word *window*. It contains the word *wind*. Windows help to keep the wind out. Try to use this method when you come across words that you do not know.

1 Look at the word *intelligent*. Write the words you recognise in the words below, then say them aloud.

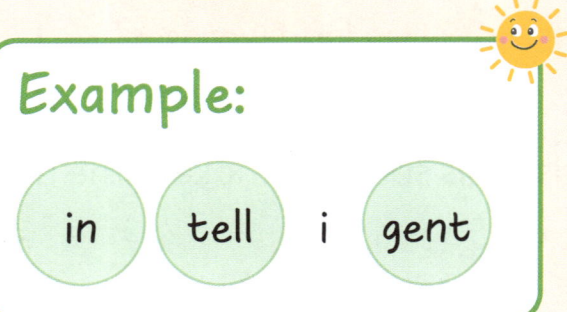

Example: in   tell   i   gent

1   suitable   _____

2   passage   _____

3   aeroplane   _____

4   birthday   _____

5   classroom   _____

6   doughnut   _____

7   earache   _____

8   football   _____

22

2 Here are some words about classroom rules:

Word box

open	do not	focus	home
closed	throw	show	note
window	slow	jokes	code

Read the words aloud to a partner in the style of a strict head teacher. Say them clearly and sternly!

3 Here are some classroom rules, but some words are missing. Select the correct word from the word box to complete each rule.

Classroom rules

Knock before entering when a door is [1]_____.

Do not [2]_____ cricket balls inside.

In class, you should stare out of the [3]_____.

When you start a lesson, [4]_____ your book.

In class, you should always [5]_____.

Let's read

This is a newspaper advert for a new school opening soon.

Super School

Begin school any time you want to before 11 a.m.

Go home any time you want to after 2 p.m.

Uniform not required.

Talking, eating and playing in class is acceptable.

At least one hour is provided for lunch and for playtime.

Homework is forbidden.

Only do the work you want to do.

You can use a dictionary to look up new words!

1. Read the advert slowly. In pairs, find out the meanings of any words that you do not know. Talk together about how you can work out the meanings of unknown words.

2. Discuss with a partner. How is Super School different to your school? Make some notes on what you discuss. Be ready to share feedback with the class.

3 Do you think Super School would be a good or a bad school to attend? Write a few sentences to explain what you think.

_____

_____

_____

4 1 Read the information in the table. Tick (✓) the school that you think each sentence applies to: your school or Super School.

Rules	Super School	My school
You must wear a uniform.		
You must listen in class.		
You do not do homework.		
You can choose the work you want to do.		
You must do the work you are given in class.		
This is a good place to learn.		
This is the school I prefer.		

2 Which school do you think should really be named Super School?
Can you explain why?

Term 1 Unit 1

Grammar builder

Look and learn

Conjunctions link words and parts of sentences together. Here are four common conjunctions:

and, **so**, **or**

- **and** is used to link something that is the same or similar without contrast:

    *His favourite lessons are English **and** Maths.*

- **so** is used to show the result of something:

    *He was very hungry, **so** he ate all the cookies.*

- **or** is used for another option:

    *Would you like orange juice **or** coke to drink?*

but

- The word **but** can be used to give conditions:

    *You can go to the beach **but** you must finish your homework first.*

- The word **but** can be used to add different information:

    *I like bananas **but** guavas are better.*

- The word **but** can be used after the words *yes* and *no* to give extra information:

    Do you like swimming?

    *Yes, **but** I prefer football. / No, **but** I can swim.*

1. In pairs, play the game *Yes, but… / No, but…* . Role play the examples before you begin. Then discuss topics 1 to 3 on page 27.

26

Example:
Do you like bananas?

Yes, but I prefer mangoes.

No, but I have to eat them because my mom says they are good for me.

1. Do you like learning English?
2. Do you think school rules are important?
3. Do you have a bike?

2. Some words have been replaced by pictures. Write out each sentence again. Fill in the words for the pictures and choose a conjunction to join the parts of each sentence.

1. I like  _____  .

   _____

2. I want to go to the  , _____ it is too far away.

   _____

3. I went to  early _____ I could practise my  .

   _____

4. I do not mind playing  _____ volleyball.

   _____

5. I do not like  , _____ I do like  .

   _____

Let's write

1 With some classmates, discuss the rules in your classroom. For example: *You must listen when others speak.*

   1 Write the rules that your class follows.

   2 With your classmates, think of two more rules of your own.

> **Extra challenge**
>
> Write two more rules of your own. In each one, use the conjunction *but*. For example: *You must do homework, but only for 20 minutes a day.*

> **Remember** ☆☆☆
>
> Make sure that you write in complete sentences and use punctuation.

Classroom rules

1 In class, you must _____.

2 In class, you must _____.

3 In class, you must _____.

4 In class, you must not _____.

5 In class, you must not _____.

6 In class, you must not _____.

7 _____

8 _____

Chapter 3

Speaking and listening

1 Read the poem out loud to a partner.

Carnival

Carnival! Carnival! Everybody shout out – Carnival!
Carnival! Carnival! Everybody shout out – Carnival!

Ah walking up de street,
Everybody dat ah meet
Jumpin' up and shoutin' 'bout Carnival.

Ah climb into de bus,
Everybody meck a fuss,
Jumpin' up an' shoutin' 'bout Carnival.

Carnival! Carnival! Everybody shout out – Carnival!
Carnival! Carnival! Everybody shout out – Carnival!

Ah step into de mall
Everybody start to bawl
Jumpin' up and shoutin' 'bout Carnival.

Ah drive down to de market
In me car, nowhere to park it.
Dey jumpin' up an' shoutin' 'bout Carnival.

Carnival! Carnival! Everybody shout out – Carnival!
Carnival! Carnival! Everybody shout out – Carnival!

Banner flyin' in de air
An de pickney dem a cheer,
Jumpin' up and shoutin' 'bout Carnival.

What a party! What a spree!
What a joyful jamboree!
Jumpin' up and shoutin' 'bout Carnival.

Carnival! Carnival! Everybody shout out – Carnival!
Carnival! Carnival! Everybody shout out – Carnival!

by Valerie Bloom

2. Circle or underline the words you notice that are Jamaican Creole words. Talk about how those words are different from English with your partner. For example, "In Creole we say *dat*, but in English we say *that*."

3. Think about the order of events in the poem. Look at the following verbs from the poem: *walking, climb, step, drive*. Write the sentence it comes from below. For example:

   <u>Ah walking up de street,</u>

   <u>Ah climb into de bus</u>

   _____

   _____

   Now retell the order of events in the poem in Standard Jamaican English to another student.

4. In a group, perform the poem to the class.

   Instructions:
   - Make sure that every person in the group reads at least one line.
   - Think of some actions for each verse to role play as the poem is read aloud.

Maybe your group could clap to the rhythm of the poem as you read!

Chapter 3

Word builder

1. Look at the poem *Carnival* from the "Speaking and listening" lesson. How does this poem make you feel? Write the words for your emotions in bubble writing or bright colours in the box below. For example, **Happy**.

ICT opportunity

Type some of your words using a computer. Can you change the colours and styles of the text?

Look and learn

Adjectives are describing words such as colours, textures and tastes.

For example:
The Jamaican flag is **black**, **green** and **gold**.
My cat's fur is **soft** and **smooth**.
This coconut ice cream is **delicious**.

2. What adjectives would you use to describe the carnival? Write them in the box.

31

Term 1 Unit 1

3 Think about the things you might see at a carnival. Write an adjective in each space to describe the noun.

_____ music   _____ costumes

_____ food   _____ people

4 Here are some words about your home and country. Read all the words in the list aloud to a partner. Can you and your partner find three words that are proper nouns? How do you recognise proper nouns?

Word box

brother	parents
English	family
Creole	live
born	home
Jamaican	country
sister	nation

Remember ☆☆☆

Proper nouns name people, animals, places or things. They always begin with capital letters.

Hi, I am Jesse.

5 Jesse has written about himself. Use the words from the word box to fill in the gaps.

My name is Jesse, I am ¹_____.

I was ²_____ in Kingston.

Now, I ³_____ in Montego Bay with my ⁴_____ and my ⁵_____.

32

Let's read

The flag of Jamaica

The flag of Jamaica has been used since 6 August 1962. The Jamaican people are very proud of their flag. It is divided into four triangles. The two triangles at the sides are coloured black for strength. The triangles at the top and bottom are green because Jamaica has a beautiful landscape. Between the triangles is a bright gold cross, just like the shining sun.

When sports players represent Jamaica at events, such as the Olympics, their clothes are the same colours as the flag. The flag usually appears on the clothes as well, for example, on the back of a jacket or on the front of a vest. When a person like an athlete wins an event, they can be seen with the flag wrapped around them. They do this because they are so proud of what they have achieved for their country.

1. Read the first paragraph again and find the word *landscape*. What do you think it means?

_____

_____

2 Read the first paragraph. Find three adjectives and write them here.

_____ _____ _____

3 Read the second paragraph. Find three nouns and write them here.

_____ _____ _____

4 Tick (✓) "True" or "False" for the below sentences.

		True	False
1	The flag is green, gold and blue.	☐	☐
2	The cross is gold like the sun.	☐	☐
3	The flag has been used since August 1952.	☐	☐
4	Jamaican sports players wear clothes in the Jamaican flag colours.	☐	☐

5 Have you ever seen the Jamaican flag flying? You may have seen it on television or in real life. What was the occasion? Write about it here.

_____

_____

_____

_____

Grammar builder

Remember ☆☆☆

Adjectives give more information about a noun or a pronoun. When we say "yellow sand", *yellow* is the adjective. When we say "two pencils", *two* is the adjective because it gives information about the pencils.

1 Read the text below.

At the zoo I saw a lion.
It was an **orange** lion.
It was an **angry**, orange lion.
It was a **wild**, angry, orange lion.
It was a **hungry**, wild, angry, orange lion.
As I stared at it, it wanted to eat me!

All the bold words are adjectives. They describe the noun *lion*. In the "Word builder" lesson, you learned that adjectives are words such as colours, textures and tastes.

With your partner, use the Adjectives box on page 36 to select three more adjectives to describe the lion.

_____   _____   _____

ICT opportunity

Use the internet to learn about a zoo in Jamaica. What are three adjectives you could use to describe the zoo?

35

Adjectives
An adjective describes a noun.

Colour	Size	Sound	Shape
blue	big	loud	egg/oval
red	small	quiet	round
green	gigantic	nice	boxy
black	short	faint	square
orange	tall	pleasant	triangular

Number	Taste	Character	Texture
few	sweet	happy	smooth
many	sour	fun-loving	rough
twenty	bitter	sad	bumpy
one	salty	clever	slimy
sixty	tangy	brave	furry

2 Underline the adjectives in these sentences.
1. My dad bought a large, hairy coconut from the market.
2. The little, black kitten played with the red ball.
3. Alias's long, curly hair looked beautiful.
4. We walked on the soft, smooth sand along the beach.
5. I always eat sweet, tangy mangoes after my dinner.

Let's write

1 You are going to write a paragraph about yourself. Plan a draft of your writing by first making notes. Write some facts about your favourite people, foods you like, games you play, the school you go to and about your friends.

Use the adjectives from the "Grammar builder" lesson to help you describe these things.

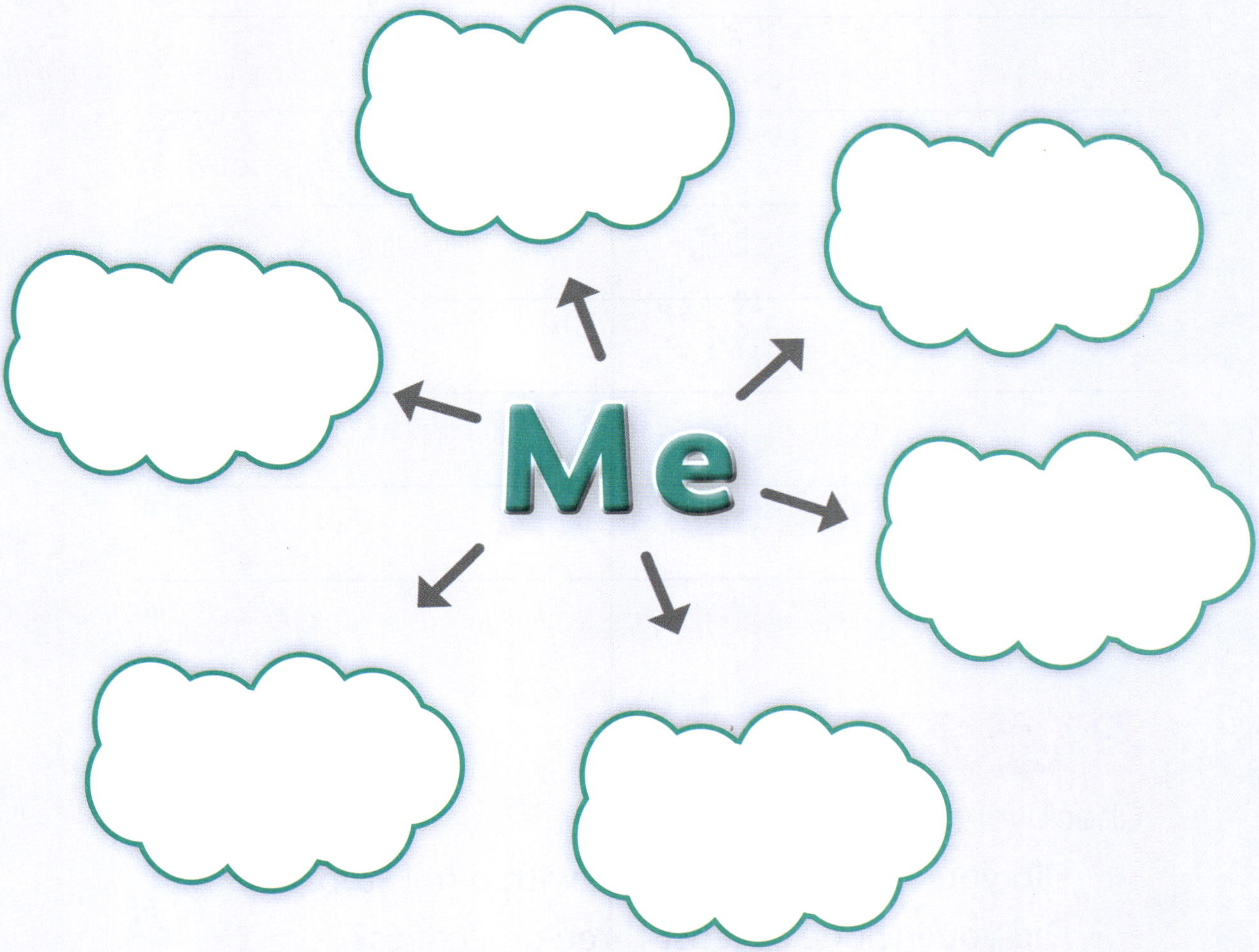

Me

2 Use the notes you have made to help you write about yourself. Write neatly and use complete sentences.

_____
_____
_____
_____
_____
_____
_____
_____
_____

Editor's checklist box ✓

Check your work when you finish.
- Did you end every sentence with a full stop?
- Did you include at least three adjectives?
- Did you use capital letters for names of people and places?

Chapter 4

Speaking and listening

1. Here are some words about your body. Stand up and read the words out loud to a partner. If a word is a body part, your partner must point to it on their own body.

   If it is not a body part, your partner can point to another student in the room or perform a mime of the word.

   Word box

leap	bleed	body
knee	cheek	male
teeth	asleep	female
feet	hairy	bone

2. Label the body parts.

t __ __ th

ch __ __ k

kn __ __

f __ __ t

3. In pairs, name five body parts that have just three letters. Discuss what these body parts do and why they are important.

Example:

toe

Your toe is part of your foot. It is important because it helps you to walk, run, jump and balance (not fall over).

What's your view?
Getting daily exercise helps you to be healthy. What kinds of exercise do you like to do?

Chapter 4

Word builder

1. Here are the words from the word box on page 39 again, but all the vowels have been left out! Complete the words with the missing vowels, then check your answers with another student.

f __ __ t

m __ l __

ch __ __ k

f __ m __ l __

b __ n __

__ sl __ __ p

2. What sounds do *pl*, *ck* and *ss* make?
Can you say some words that begin with *pl*?
Can you say some words that end with *ck* or *ss*?
Say the words below out loud to your partner.

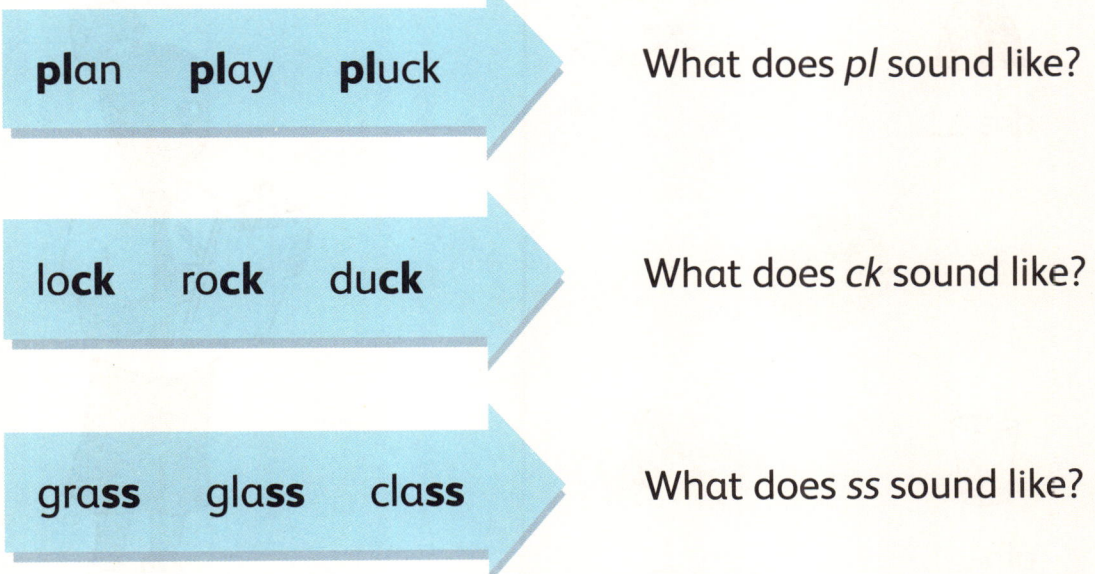

plan   **pl**ay   **pl**uck   What does *pl* sound like?

lo**ck**   ro**ck**   du**ck**   What does *ck* sound like?

gra**ss**   gla**ss**   cla**ss**   What does *ss* sound like?

Can you and your partner think of more words that begin with *pl* or end with *ck* or *ss*?

3 Write in the missing letters, then blend and read each word one by one to your partner.

__ um 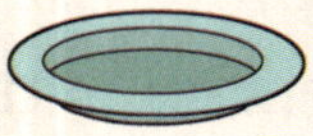   __ ate

pl

__ ant    __ ay

ti  __   ki __

ck

bla  __   clo __

dre  __   ki __

ss

gla  __   pre __

Let's read

Look and learn

The words *inside* and *outside* are called **prepositions**. Prepositions tell you where things are. For example: *My hair is **on** my head.*

Parts of the body

Some parts of the body you can see, but other parts of the body you cannot see because they are inside you. These parts are called *internal organs*. *Internal* is another word for *inside*.

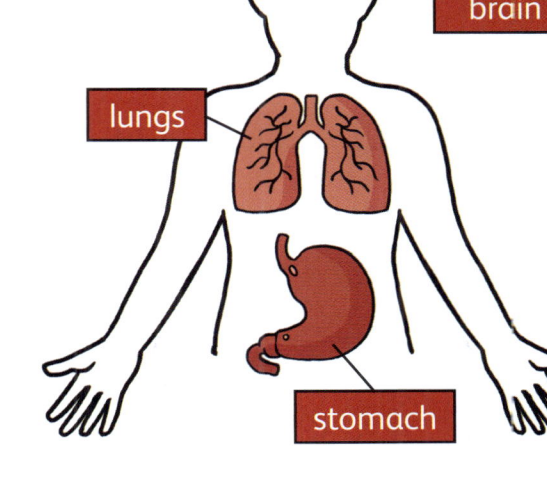

The body has lots of important internal organs that help to keep you alive, so it is important to look after your body, inside and out!

Inside your chest there are two lungs. You use these to breathe. Inside your head is your brain. You use this to think. Inside your tummy is your stomach. You use this to digest the food you eat.

1 Read the text on previous page and answer the questions.

1 What two-word phrase is used to describe parts of the body that are inside you?

_____

2 What part of the body helps you to breathe?

_____

3 Why can you not see your stomach? Use a preposition in your answer.

_____

4 Write two things that your brain could help you to do today.

_____

_____

5 Why do you think it is important to look after your body?

_____

_____

ICT opportunity

Use a computer to find out the names of two more internal organs. What do they do?

Grammar builder

Remember ☆☆☆

Adjectives are words used to give more information about a noun, which could be a person, place or an object. Adjectives include words for colours, sizes and shapes. Here are some examples:
- *Lara has **brown** eyes.*
- *Benjamin is **tall**.*
- *She has **curly** hair.*

Look and learn

Adjectives are also used to compare one item to another. To do this, we usually add **-er** to the end of the adjective.
- *Benjamin is tall but Peter is tall**er**.*

For adjectives that end in a **-y**, change the **y** to an **i** and then add **-er** to the end of the adjective.
- *She has curly hair but mine is curl**ier**.*

These adjectives are called **comparatives**.

1 Complete the sentences using the correct form of the adjective in brackets.

  1 John is _____ than Bob. (strong)

  2 An elephant is _____ than a lion. (heavy)

  3 Mangoes are _____ than lemons. (sweet)

  4 A mouse is _____ than a rabbit. (tiny)

Look and learn

We also use adjectives to say what comes top or bottom of a group by adding **-est** to the end of the adjective.

For adjectives that end in a **-y**, change the **y** to an **i** and then add **-est** to the end of the adjective.

For example:
- *Peter is taller than Benjamin, but David is the tall**est**.*
- *My hair is curlier than hers, but yours is the curl**iest**.*

These adjectives are called **superlatives**.

Be careful! Not all adjectives follow the same pattern.

For example:
- *Eating fruit once every day is **good**, but twice a day is **better** and three times a day is **best**.*
- *Eating chocolate once every day is **bad**, but twice a day is **worse** and three times a day is **the worst**.*

These adjectives are called **superlatives**.

Remember ☆☆☆

When you change the ending of a word and add a new ending, the new ending is called an **inflectional ending**. Inflectional endings create another form of the same word. In Activity 2 on page 47, the adjectives become comparative or superlative words when you add the new ending.

2 Complete the sentences by writing the correct adjective from the word box.

Word box

curlier   bigger   better   tallest   faster

1 My brother has big feet but my Dad's are _____.

2 Joe is the _____ boy in the class.

3 Lara's hair is _____ than Kendra's.

4 Drinking apple juice is _____ than drinking cola.

5 Can anyone run _____ than Usain Bolt?

Term 1 Unit 1

Let's write

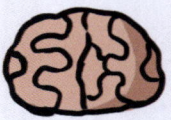

Brain

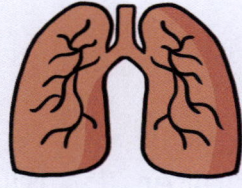

Lungs

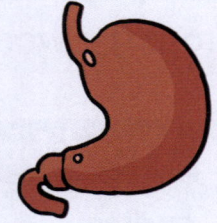

Stomach

1. Work in a small group. Choose one of the body parts shown in the pictures and plan a short presentation to give to your class. Try to use adjectives to describe the body part you choose.

   Use this space to plan your presentation.

   Introduction: Hello / thank everyone for listening / outline what your group will present.

   _____
   _____
   _____
   _____

   Middle: Where the body part you have chosen is located.

   _____
   _____
   _____
   _____

What the body part does for you.

_____

_____

_____

Why it is important to take care of it.

_____

_____

_____

End: Remind everyone what your group's presentation was about and ask your classmates to ask your group some questions.

_____

_____

_____

_____

2. Listen to the presentations given by your classmates. For two of the presentations, think of a question that you could ask. Write your questions here:

First question: _____

Second question: _____

Chapter 5

 **Speaking and listening**

Prepare to read, write and listen to a healthy haiku!

> **Look and learn**
> All words can be broken down into **syllables**. Short words may have just one or two syllables, but longer words can have more. A syllable is a sound or a beat. The best way to recognise syllables is to say a word out loud, slowly. Here are some examples:
> - *Six* has one syllable: *six*
> - *Seven* has two syllables: *sev-en*
> - *Eleven* has three syllables: *e-lev-en*

A **haiku** is a type of Japanese poem that is only three lines long. Haiku poems have 17 syllables in total; five syllables in the first line, seven in the second line and five in the third.

Haiku poems almost never rhyme. Haiku poems can contain adjectives to give descriptions. Look out for the adjectives in the poems below.

1. Here are some haiku poems about food. Read them out loud and count the syllables.

Yummy Berries
Juicy red berries,
Ripe, cold and sweet in my mouth.
I eat them all up.

Dinner Time
Smell the hot chicken.
Spices fill the smoky air.
Dinner time is here.

Chapter 5

2 Write your own haiku poem about food and draw a picture to go with it.

My healthy haiku poem:

Title: _____

_____

_____

_____

_____

3 Read your haiku poem to a partner. Listen to your partner's haiku poem.

51

Word builder

1 Here are some words about healthy eating. Read the first word and remember how to spell it. Then write it in your notebook without looking at the word here. Do the same for all the words. When you finish, ask a partner to check if your spelling is correct.

Word box

icing	ripe	bite	knife
ice cream	rice	lime	fried
life	like	slice	pie

2 Read the words out loud to your partner. Can you find any nouns? Think of adjectives to describe the nouns you found.

3 Choose six words from the list that have one syllable. Write them down in alphabetical order.

_____

_____

_____

_____

_____

4 Some words are missing from this story. Use the words in the list to fill in the gaps.

One day, Dad was preparing a picnic. He made his favourite dish of [1]_____ and peas and put it in a bowl. Mom had made fresh lemon [2]_____. Dad was hungry and the smell was yummy! Dad got a [3]_____ and cut himself a big [4]_____. He ate it all up with some vanilla [5]_____. When Mom saw what Dad had done, she was not happy, but Dad made her smile when he said it was the best pie he had ever eaten in his [6]_____.

5 Think about eating a meal with your family. Write two sentences about it. Each sentence must contain at least one of the words from the word box on page 52.

1 _____

2 _____

Term 1 Unit 1

Let's read

1   Read this passage about food and answer the questions.

Some foods are healthy, and some foods are less healthy. Fruit and vegetables are very healthy. These foods contain lots of vitamins and minerals that your body needs to help it work. Chocolate, soda and cakes are less healthy because they contain a lot of sugar and fat. These foods should only be eaten as a treat. If you eat too much unhealthy food, it can cause illness. This is why it is important to have a balanced diet that includes plenty of healthy food, so you can still have an occasional treat.

1   Name two healthy foods that are mentioned.

_____ and _____

2   What do the healthy foods contain which makes them good for you?

_____ and _____

Chapter 5

3   Name two unhealthy foods that are mentioned.

    _____ and _____

4   What do the unhealthy foods contain which makes them bad for you?

    _____ and _____

5   Why is it important not to eat too many of the less healthy foods?

    _____

6   When is it OK to eat the less healthy foods?

    _____

What's your view?
Should you only eat fruits and vegetables, or is it okay to eat cake, too?

7   Do you think you have a balanced diet? Explain your answer.

    _____

    _____

Grammar builder

Some words are very useful because they help you to show others exactly what you want.

I want this pineapple, please.

In the picture, the girl does not want just any pineapple, she wants one particular pineapple. She uses the words **this** *pineapple*. Here are some more examples:

I like this hat.

I want that car.

You need to read these books.

Pick up those bags!

1   Look at the pictures carefully and read the speech bubbles. Identify which of these words are used in each one and circle it:

Word box

this   that   these   those

The words *this*, *that*, *these*, *those* are called **demonstratives**.

Look at the examples again. Do you notice a pattern?

The words *this* and *that* can only be used to refer to one item: *this hat*, *that car*.
- *This* refers to something near you.
- *That* refers to something not near you.

The words *these* and *those* are used when there is more than one item: *these books*, *those bags*.
- *These* refer to things near you.
- *Those* refer to things not near you.

2 Write the correct demonstrative from *this*, *that*, *these* or *those*.

1 Fay likes _____ colour.

2 My Granny made _____ pies.

3 The noise came from _____ tree.

4 Where did _____ cat go?

5 Who wants _____ sweets?

3 Write two sentences of your own that contain at least one demonstrative.

1 _____

2 _____

Let's write

1. Fill in your food diary for one day. Write in the foods you eat at mealtimes and any snacks you have in between. Be careful to put the foods in the correct column!

My food diary

Time of day	Fruits or vegetables	Other healthy food	Less healthy treats
Breakfast			
Morning snack			
Lunch			
Afternoon snack			
Dinner			
Evening snack			
Supper			

2. Did you eat mostly healthy food or mostly unhealthy food?

   _____

   _____

3. Compare your diary to a friend's food diary. Talk about how they are similar or different.

Remember, you can use the conjunction *but* or **comparative adjectives** to make comparisons.

4 Do you think your diary would be the same or different on another day of the week? Do you eat differently at the weekends or during holidays?

_____

_____

_____

5 In pairs or a small group, plan a well-balanced menu for a family for a weekend. In the family, there is Mom, Dad and two children aged six and nine.

Chapter 6

Speaking and listening

1. Look back at the "Let's write" lesson in Chapter 4. Your group prepared a presentation on a topic related to looking after your body. Discuss with your group the answers to the following questions.

   1. What words describe how you felt during the presentation?

      Example:
      I felt really nervous. I was too scared to make eye contact...

   2. Did you enjoy giving the presentation? Say why or why not. Tell your group why you felt the way you did.

      Example:
      I enjoyed giving the presentation. It was very interesting and I liked answering the questions from our classmates at the end.

   3. How did other people in class respond to your presentation?

      Example:
      All my classmates were very kind, but I think I need to work on my body language.

2 Look back at the "Let's write" lesson in Chapter 4. You listened to the presentations of other groups in your class. Discuss with your group the answers to the following questions.

1. What words describe how you felt when you were listening to other presentations?

> **Example:**
> I was really interested in the first two presentations, but after that I became bored.

2. Did you enjoy listening to your classmates? Can you say why?

3. Did you ask any questions? Tell your group what questions you asked.

Word builder

Here are some words about taking care of yourself:

Word box

grow	throw	smile	child
time	nail	elbow	human
baby	old	lady	spine

1 Read the words aloud to a partner. For each word, ask your partner to do a mime to match the word.

2 Choose a word from the word box to fill in the gaps in each sentence. You cannot use any word more than once.

1 The _____ had a beautiful _____.

2 A _____ will _____ into a _____.

3 The _____ is a bone in the _____ body.

3 Sort the words from the word box into nouns, verbs and adjectives.

Nouns	Verbs	Adjectives

Extra challenge

Three words could be a noun or a verb. Do you know which words they are?

4 What sounds do *fl*, *pr* and *gr* make? Can you say some words that begin with *fl*, *pr* or *gr*?

Say the words below out loud to your partner.

flan   **fl**ap   **fl**ea   What does *fl* sound like?

prom   **pr**ay   **pr**am   What does *pr* sound like?

grape   **gr**aph   **gr**andparents   What does *gr* sound like?

Can you and your partner think of more words that begin with *fl*, *pr* and *gr*? Use a dictionary or online tool for more ideas.

_____   _____   _____

_____   _____   _____

Let's read

1 Read this paragraph about teeth and answer the comprehension questions.

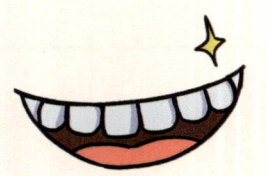

You use your teeth to chew food. Babies are born without teeth; they cannot chew food. Teeth start to grow through the gums when a baby is about six months old. As the baby grows, more teeth come through until there are 20 teeth. All children have ten teeth on the bottom and ten teeth on the top. These teeth are sometimes called *milk teeth*. When a child is about six or seven, some of the milk teeth can start to feel loose. This is because adult teeth are starting to push through. Milk teeth fall out naturally and are replaced by adult teeth. There are more adult teeth than milk teeth; an adult has 32 teeth in total. You can look after your teeth by brushing them twice a day with toothpaste and by visiting the dentist.

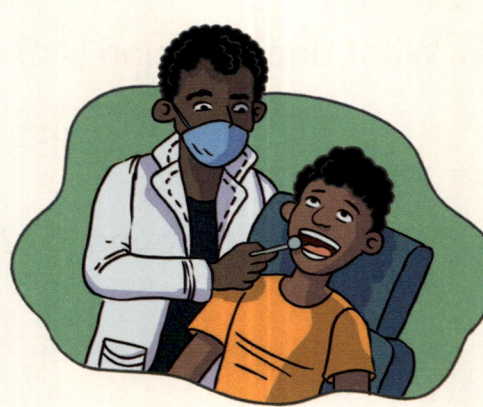

1   How many teeth do children and adults have?
    Children: _____   Adults: _____

2   What are children's teeth sometimes called?
    _____

3   List two things you should do to look after your teeth.
    _____

2   Think about adjectives you could use to describe healthy teeth. Write as many adjectives as you can on the tube of toothpaste.

Remember ☆☆☆

Adjectives add more detail to a noun.

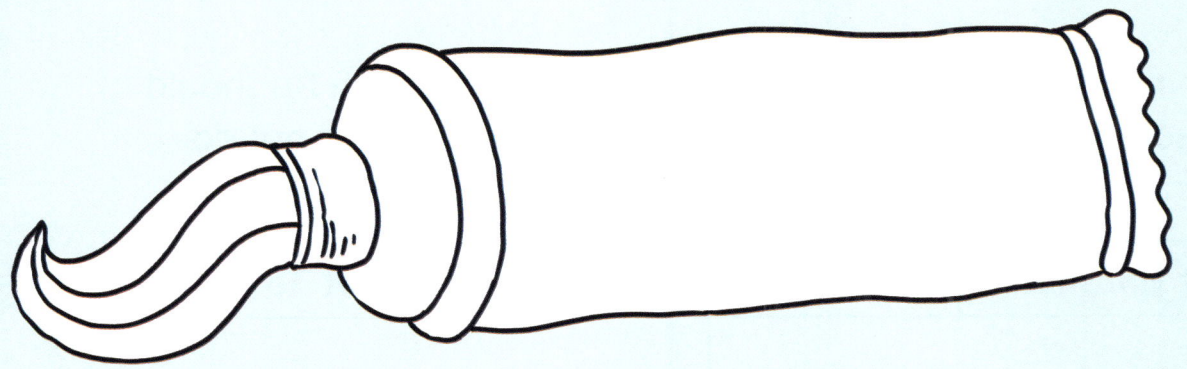

Term 1 Unit 1

Grammar builder

L👀k and learn

Using the word *not*

Look at the pictures and read the information about taking care of yourself.

This is very healthy.

This is **not** very healthy.

Eat lots of healthy food.

Do **not** eat too much unhealthy food.

1 Think of three tips for taking care of yourself. Each tip should also have an opposite – something that you should not do. Write each tip and its opposite in the table.

What you should do	What you should not do

2 Compare your tips with a partner. Talk about different things you should do and should not do to stay healthy.

> **Remember** ☆ ☆ ☆
>
> In Chapter 4, you learned that the words *inside* and *outside* are called **prepositions**.
> Words like *on, under, in, behind* and *between* are also prepositions.
> A preposition is a word that shows the location of a noun.

3 My little brother always forgets where he puts his things. Read the text and tell your partner what you think he has lost.

Hmm … where did I put it? Where could it be?

It is not there **on** the table.

 It is not **under** my bed.

It is not **in** my toy box.

No, it is not **behind** the toy box.

 And it is not **between** my books.

Look around the class and take turns with your partner to say where things or people are or are not.

Example:
The teacher is sitting **on** the chair.
The dictionaries are **between** the window and the door.

Let's write

Complete this task with a partner or small group. Choose one of these topics related to looking after your body:

looking after your teeth　　　getting exercise　　　eating well

1. Prepare a short presentation for your class about the topic you have chosen.

   Include these facts:
   - Why you have chosen the topic.
   - Why it is important to do this for your body to stay healthy.
   - What might happen if you do not do this to try to stay healthy.

   Make your presentation lively and interesting. Maybe you could use a computer for the presentation. Think about including some of these things:
   - pictures
   - drama or a role play
   - poetry or a song about your topic.

   If you are working in a group, you must make sure that every person has a job to do. Everybody should take part in the presentation. For example, share out the bullet point tasks between different people. This is called "teamwork".

Use this space to plan your presentation.

2 Now, neatly write up what you will say in the presentation.

_____

_____

_____

_____

_____

_____

3 Give your presentation to the class.

Remember ☆☆☆

Speak slowly, in a loud, clear voice, but do not shout. At the end, remember to ask if anybody has any questions for you.

Term 1 Unit 1 Review and assessment

Speaking and listening

1. Work with your partner. Take turns to choose three body parts from the word box and describe what you think they look like on you, to your partner.

Word box

legs	toes	toes	mouth	hair
head	arms	nose	body	eyes
face	fingers	ears		

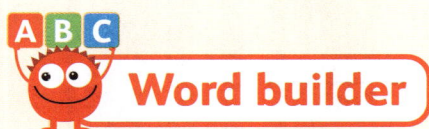
Word builder

1. Complete the table.

Adjective	Comparative	Superlative
		happiest
	bigger	
	heavier	
sad		
		darkest
clean		

Review and assessment

Let's read

1. Circle and correct the ten punctuation errors in the paragraph. Then answer the questions below.

> My name is nathan. my mom and I are planning my birthday party for next Month. She asked me what kinds of food I wanted. i told her that I wanted lots of soda, chips, chocolate chip cookies and candy She said we could have only Two of those things, but I also had to think of some Healthy snacks that my friends would enjoy. At first, I could not think of any and I was sure my friends would not have fun at my party Then my mom reminded me that I like nuts and fruits. She said maybe my friends do too. She was right, my friends eat these things all the time. Now, at my party, we are going to have soda cookies, sandwiches, peanuts, cashews and a fruit and cheese platter. There will also be my race car cake, it is my Birthday after all.

1. Nathan wanted soda and _____ at his party.
   a   salad   b   candy   c   chicken
2. How did he feel when he could not think of snacks his friends would enjoy?
3. What proved that Nathan's mother was right when she said his friends would also enjoy some healthy snacks?
4. How did Nathan feel at the end?

71

Grammar builder

1 Use the conjunctions in the word box to complete each sentence.

Word box

but   so   or   and

1. I like potato chips _____ fruits are better for me.

2. Dancing _____ playing cricket are fun things to do.

3. Jeremy wants either a basketball _____ a football for his birthday.

4. I missed the bus _____ I had to walk home.

5. Daniel _____ Candice are coming to my party.

Let's write

1 You want to write a letter to a new friend. First, write some facts about yourself. Include the foods you like, the games you play and the name of your school. Make sure you use adjectives to describe these things.

_____

_____

_____

_____

TERM 1

Unit 2

Chapter 7

 **Speaking and listening**

 I have great news today! My cousin had a baby last night. It was a little boy called Jamal. My family are all very happy!

 Wow! That is lovely news!

1. What news do you have from your own family or community today? Write your news below.

2 What news do other people in class have today? Ask two students in your class. Write their news.

News from _____

_____

News from _____

_____

3 Choose one of the news stories. Draw a picture of the event. Label the important items or people in your picture. Tell the class about your news report.

Example:

This is a picture of Josh's new bicycle. It has two wheels and is red. He found it wrapped up as a surprise last weekend at home. Yes, it was his birthday and his parents bought it for him as a gift.

Word builder

1 Here are some words taken from news stories. Read each word to a partner, but whisper as if you are passing on a secret message.

Word box

story	brother	flower	stain
great	promise	blow	flew
crime	sleep	please	green

2 Choose one of the words from the word box to complete each sentence.

1 The boy made a _____ to pay back the money.

2 A woman was rescued from the sea by her _____.

3 The children said it was the best _____ they had ever heard.

4 The thief drove away in a _____ car.

5 People in the town are worried about _____.

Remember ☆☆☆

If you do not know the meaning of new words, you can look them up in a dictionary.

3 Choose a word from the word box on page 75 that was not used in Activity 2. Write a sentence of your own.

_____

_____

4 1 Take turns with a partner to say the words below out loud and state the number of syllables in each word. For example: *Mango has two syllables*.

2 Find new words within words and write them below. The first one is done for you. Compare your answers with a partner.

mango   <u>man, an, go</u>

small   _____

sink   _____

person   _____

tomato   _____

cattle   _____

great   _____

farm   _____

pencil   _____

carpet   _____

donkey   _____

snail   _____

Let's read

1. How do you know about events that are happening? Name three different ways to find out about interesting or important events. For example: *I know about important events from the television.*

   _____

   _____

   _____

- News reports tell you important information about an event: what happened, to whom it happened, when and where it happened and why or how it happened.
- News reports often have a picture. Here are three pictures from news reports:

A

Storm damage

B

Sporting success

C

Community matters

2 With your partner, discuss what is happening in each picture. Look for the important information. Talk about why you think each event has made the news.

3 With your partner, make lists of words related to each picture. Use:
- **nouns** for items you can see
- **adjectives** to describe the nouns
- **verbs** to describe the actions that are happening.

Some words for picture A have been added for you.

A – Storm damage	B – Sporting success	C – Community matters
a cracked white house the house is falling over high waves are splashing rough sea stones flood		

4 Find two examples of news reports with a picture. You could look in a newspaper, such as *The Children's Own*, a magazine or online.
- Cut out (or print) the two pictures so that the pictures are separated from the reports.
- Cut out (or print) the two reports.
- Give your partner one of the pictures. Ask them to describe it to you in detail.
- Now show your partner the two reports. Ask your partner to identify which report matches the picture they have described. Then swap over.

Grammar builder

News stories need to include a lot of detail. Details are added to news stories by using nouns and adjectives.

> **Remember** ☆ ☆ ☆
>
> **Adjectives** describe nouns. In most sentences, adjectives are placed before the noun they describe. For example: *I wore a **blue** shirt.*

1. Choose one of the news reports you used for Activity 4 in the "Let's read" lesson. Stick it on this page. Then complete these tasks:
   1. Find all the nouns in the news story and shade them in a colour of your choice.
   2. Find all the adjectives in the news story and shade them in another colour.

2 You can use adjectives to improve your writing by adding details. Rewrite each of these sentences. When you rewrite them, expand each sentence by adding at least two adjectives. For example: *The thief was wearing blue jeans…*

1 The thief was wearing jeans, a T-shirt and a baseball cap.

_____

2 In Greenville, there are many houses, a park, a school and a shop.

_____

3 Rain will continue for the next week and there is a risk of flooding in places.

_____

ICT opportunity

Use a computer to draw a picture showing one of your sentences with adjectives.

Let's write

1. You are going to write your own news story based on this picture.

Instructions

Your report should be one paragraph long. You should include the essential facts: what happened, when, where, who was involved and why or how it happened.

1. Prepare a first draft by making notes in the frame below. This does not need to be in complete sentences, it can include notes and helpful words that you might use.

What / When	winner of 100 metres race / last Friday
Where	
Who	
Why / How	

2 Write your report neatly. You should write in complete sentences.

- The awards celebration for _____ happened last Friday.
  _____

- It took place at _____ School _____ (in the school hall / the school assembly room, etc.)
  _____

- There were many people there. They included _____ (parents, teachers, friends…)
  _____

- The awards celebration took place because _____ (students passed their exams… / did well in their sport… / helped people in their community, etc.)
  _____

- The headmaster said it is very important to have award celebrations because _____
  _____.

> **Editor's checklist box** ✓
>
> Check your work when you finish.
> - Have you included full stops and capital letters?

3. Read your news story again. Can you find a way to expand your writing by adding details? Look for sentences where you could add adjectives.

> **Example:**
> The awards show for the students with the highest exam results happened last Friday. The **amazing** awards show for the **fantastic, hard-working** students with the highest exam results happened last Friday.

Rewrite the sentences here with more adjectives and details:

_____

_____

_____

_____

Chapter 8

 **Speaking and listening**

When something belongs to you, it means that you own it. You are the owner. When you own something special, it is your job to look after it and keep it safe. It might be a pet, a special toy, an item in your house or even a plant in your garden.

This is a photograph of my great-grandparents. It is very special because I never met them when they were alive and I like to hear stories about them.

This is my mother's necklace. It is very special because it was a gift from my father when they were married.

Do you own something special or is there something special that belongs to someone in your family?

1. Draw a picture or stick a photograph of the item in the left box on page 85.

2 Make some notes to say why your item is special.

Example:
- old pocket watch
- father's watch – belonged to his father
- special birthday gift

	• • •

3 Use your notes to talk to your classmates about the special item. Explain why it is special to you. Answer questions from your classmates about your item.

4 Listen to your classmates talk about their special items. Then think of one or two questions to ask your classmates about their item.

ICT opportunity

Make a presentation on a computer about your special item. Type some information about what it is and why it is special. Try to find a picture that looks like your special item.

Word builder

1. Here are some words that you could use for describing special items:

   Word box

place	precious	crack	break
plastic	flat	crystal	black
prize	flash	bracelet	blue

   Read the words aloud to a partner. Circle any words you do not know and use a dictionary or online tool to look up their meaning.

2. Some items have been found in a treasure chest. The descriptions of the items are incomplete. Choose one of the words from the word box to complete each description.

   - A beautiful silver _____ .
   - A broken china pot with a large _____ on the handle.
   - A clear _____ vase that glistens in the sunlight.
   - Some _____ gold coins that are over 400 years old.

3 Imagine that you work in a museum and you have lots of interesting items to display. Write three sentences to describe items that you have. You must use at least one of the words from the word box on page 86 in each sentence.

1 _____

2 _____

3 _____

4 Look at the following consonant blends:

pl	bl	fl	pr	br	cr

Write the words in Activity 1 under the correct consonant blend. Add two more words of your own to each blend. Compare your words with a partner.

Let's read

1 Read this story about *Show and Tell*.

The children brought special items to school for *Show and Tell*. Carl had his toy car, Paula had her party dress and Fiona had her netball trophy. Harry watched the other children stand up and talk one by one. Harry brought Bumpy Bear, a soft toy bear that he had had since he was born. Bumpy was Harry's best friend. Harry held Bumpy up for the class to see and started talking. Suddenly, three boys began laughing and pointing at Harry. "He is a baby!", Carl said. "He is friends with a toy!", another called out. "And the toy is old and dirty!" called the third boy, as he pointed to a patch on the bear's belly. Harry was very upset and began to cry. The teacher told off the boys for being so mean to Harry. Paula and Fiona went to comfort Harry. "Do not worry!" said Paula. "We love Bumpy, too", said Fiona, and she hugged Bumpy. Harry, Paula and Fiona became best friends and the unkind boys never bothered them again.

2 Write some adjectives to describe these characters:

Harry	Carl	Fiona and Paula

3 Discuss the questions with your partner. Make some notes about your ideas to share with the class.

1   Why did Carl said Harry was like a baby?

   _____

2   Do you think Carl is a kind person? Why?

   _____

3   What do you think about Fiona and Paula? Why?

   _____

4   What can we learn from this story?

   _____

Term 1 Unit 2

Grammar builder

You have been learning about **adjectives**. Adjectives describe nouns. Adjectives allow you to be very specific and to give lots of detail.

Reading would be very boring without adjectives!

1 Look at these three pictures and write as many adjectives as you can think of to describe each picture.

A

B

C

Picture A	Picture B	Picture C
pink		

2 Choose one of the pictures. Write three sentences to describe what you can see. Include as many adjectives as you can.

1 _____

2 _____

3 _____

3 Circle all of the adjectives you have used in your sentences. How many did you use?

_____

Let's write

Two children wrote sentences to describe the special items that they took to school for *Show and Tell*. Read their descriptions:

1 I have brought a vase. It is wooden with some patterns on the outside. It belongs to my gran. You can put flowers in it.

2 I have brought in a picture of a gold bracelet that belongs to my lovely mother. It has shiny stones like diamonds as well as sparkly red stones called *rubies*. It is very heavy and is too big for me to wear. She keeps it in a black box. The box has a soft velvet cushion inside and it locks shut for safe keeping.

The second piece of writing is more interesting because there are a lot of adjectives. When you are reading, adjectives help you to imagine what something is like.

1. Improve the first description by rewriting it. Expand it by adding some adjectives. You should write four complete sentences.

_____

_____

_____

Chapter 8

_____

_____

_____

2 Choose item 1 or 2 on page 92 and draw a colourful picture of it.

3 Show your picture to your partner and ask them to check how well your picture matches the written description of the item.

Chapter 9

Speaking and listening

Read this paragraph about what Lea did last weekend.

Last weekend it was Lea's seventh birthday. She went with her mom and two friends to visit Hope Zoo. They got up very early in the morning and set off for the zoo. At the zoo they saw lions, monkeys, snakes and beautiful birds, too.
They ate a picnic lunch and spent all day smiling, laughing and watching the animals. At six o'clock they went home for dinner and told their families about their wonderful day.

Remember ☆☆☆

A **summary** is a short version of a story containing only the **essential** facts. It does not have many extra details or specific information.

1. Underline the parts of the paragraph that you think are essential facts. Talk to your partner. Did you both underline the same parts of the story?

   Use the parts that you underlined to tell your partner a summary of what Lea did last weekend.

2 Now ask your partner to tell you about what they did last weekend. Listen carefully to their story. When your partner has finished, write a summary of their story in the box below.

3 Now read your summary to your partner.

Word builder

Here are some words that you see often when you are reading:

Word box

called	could	from	have
just	long	many	most
other	some	there	where

1. Read the words aloud slowly to a partner. Then listen to your partner read them back to you. Next, read them to a partner again, but read them more quickly. Keep swapping over until you read them as quickly as you can. Who can read them the quickest, you or your partner?

2. In pairs, complete the sentences with a word from the word box above.

   1. _____ is my book?

   2. I spoke to Leroy five minutes ago. I _____ spoke to him.

   3. Anna has so _____ pets, her house is like a zoo.

   4. I _____ three brothers and one sister.

   5. I come _____ Jamaica.

6 _____ are five pencils in my pencil case.

7 Hanna needs to cut her hair. It is too _____.

8 I have too many sweets. Do you want _____?

9 My teacher _____ my name out when she did the register.

10 Rhona is the _____ popular girl in the class.

11 My mom could not swim when she was six years old, but I _____.

12 I do not want that book. I want the _____ one.

3 In groups of three or four, take turns to choose a word from the word box on page 96 and spell it out loud. The other group members must not look at the words. The first group member to say the correct word gets a point. The winner is the student with the most points by the end of the game.

> **What's your view?**
> Can you think of any other words that you use every day? Do you know how to spell them?

Let's read

This story has two parts. With your partner, take turns to each read a part of the story out loud.

Peter's playtime

Part One

Peter was playing ball in the street with his friends. The Sun was shining high in the sky and the birds chirped sweetly in the trees. Peter ran to catch the ball and suddenly he fell over. He cried out loudly because he hurt his ankle. There was a small hole in the pavement, and he did not see it in time. Peter's friend called for his mom to come quickly.

Part Two

Peter's mom arrived and picked Peter up off the floor. She carried him home and sat him on a chair. She raised his leg slowly and rested his ankle on another chair. "You need something cold to put on it." she said and went to the freezer. She came back with some frozen food wrapped in a towel and put it carefully on Peter's ankle. She hugged Peter warmly and he stopped crying. "Thank you, Mom. You are the best!" Peter said.

1. Look at the pictures on next page. Number them in the order that they happened in the story.

2 Read the text again. Discuss the questions with your class.
1. How do you think Peter felt when he fell over?
2. What are some adjectives that could describe Peter's mom? Explain how you chose these adjectives.
3. How can we be a good friend when someone hurts themselves?

3 Sometimes a text can be separated by a **heading**. A heading is like a title – it tells you what the text is about. Write a heading for each part of the text to be used in place of "Part One" and "Part Two".

Part One: _____

Part Two: _____

4 What do you think happened to Peter next? Talk to a partner. Then share your ideas with the class.

Term 1 Unit 2

Grammar builder

Verbs and tenses

1 Look back at the story in the "Let's read" lesson on page 98. Find as many verbs in the story as you can and circle them

How many verbs did you find? _____

Look more closely at the verbs you circled. What do you notice? Discuss this with a partner and make some notes.

_____
_____
_____

The story was about something that has already happened. It is not going to happen in the future, and it is not happening right now. The story happened in **the past**.

L👀k and learn

There are three main tenses: the **past**, the **present** and the **future**.

Maggie **went** to the beach.	Past tense
Maggie **will** go to the beach.	Future tense
Maggie **goes** to the beach.	Present tense

Most of the verbs in the story are in the **past tense**. You can recognise past tense verbs because they often end in **-d** or **-ed**. Be careful though; some verbs do not follow this pattern. Verbs that do not follow this pattern are called **irregular verbs**, for example the verbs **to be (was)** and **to go (went)**.

100

2 Look at these sentences. Tick (✓) if they are in the past, present or future tense.

	Past	Present	Future
My father works in an office.			
On holiday, I will swim every day.			
We all ate hamburgers and watched the game.			

3 Here are some sentences in the past tense. Choose a verb from the word box to complete each one.

Word box

sailed   watched   went   kicked   was

1   Jada _____ the ball.

2   Most of the day _____ sunny.

3   Many people _____ the cricket match.

4   The boat _____ out from the bay.

5   I _____ to the market with Mom.

Remember ☆☆☆

When you change the ending of a word and add a new ending, the new ending is called an **inflectional ending**. Inflectional endings create another form of the same word.

Let's write

Do you remember what you did on your last birthday or on another special day? For example, Christmas or Easter, or somebody else's birthday?

You are going to write a short paragraph about what you did on that special day. Look back at the story in the "Speaking and listening" lesson about Lea's birthday to help you.

Remember ☆☆☆

You are writing about something that happened in the past, so your verbs need to be in the **past tense**.

1. Prepare your first draft by making notes in the table below:

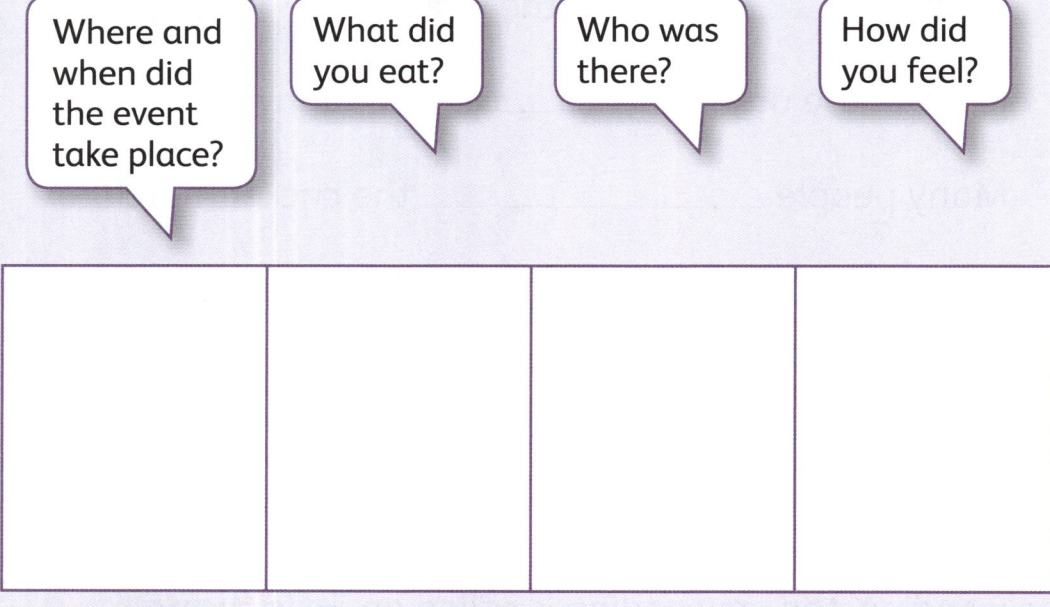

2 Write your story neatly.

_____
_____
_____
_____
_____
_____
_____
_____

Editor's checklist box ✓

Check your work when you finish.
- Have you used full stops and capital letters?
- Are the verbs in the past tense?
- Have you used adjectives to add detail?

Now, read your story to a classmate and ask them to summarise it.

Term 1 Unit 2

Chapter 10

Speaking and listening

A **headline** is a short, catchy sentence at the start of a news report. A headline is like a heading. It tells us what the story is about. It grabs our attention.

1. Choose a headline to match each news story. Write the headline in the box above each picture.
   - Jewel thief caught
   - A lucky ticket
   - Going for gold
   - Local artist wins national prize

2 Think about news stories that you have heard, seen or read recently. For example: *Department store in Mobay damaged by fire* or *Usain Bolt wins again*.

Draw a picture to go with a news story that you know about. Write a headline to go with your picture.

Headline:

Picture:

3 Talk to a partner about your news story. Tell them what happened. Answer any questions your partner has.

4 Listen to your partner's news story. Ask them questions if you are not sure about any of the events in the story.

Word builder

Word box

group	slip	dream	friend
ground	stops	drive	skate
slow	storm	from	skeleton

1. Read the words aloud to a partner in the style of a newsreader on TV or radio. Make sure that you pronounce the start and end of every word clearly.

2. Here is a paragraph from a news story. Some words are missing. Find a word from the word box to fill in each gap.

Weather chaos

A strong _____ hit the town of Greenville last night. Trees have been ripped from the _____ by strong winds and people _____ the area were evacuated. They will be able to return home when the rain _____ falling.

Chapter 10

3 Choose one of the headlines below. Write your own short news story to go with it. Choose three words from the Word box on p102 and use them in your story.

"Dinosaur bone discovery"; "Traffic trouble"; "Once in a lifetime".

_____

_____

_____

_____

_____

4 Write out each new word from the word box on page 106 in the correct column in the table.

sk	dr	fr	gr	st	sl

Choose three words that you think are the hardest to learn. Write them out again as a spelling pyramid. This is where you start a new line and add a new letter to the word each time, for example:

b
bl
blu
blue

Let's read

1 Read this newspaper article slowly. Then answer the questions below.

Go bananas!

The Minister for Health visited a Portland banana plantation today to tell families to eat more bananas. He believes this will help to improve the health of children.

Bananas are grown across Jamaica on plantations large and small. They are easy to find and buy in any shop or market.

The banana is at its best when the skin becomes bright yellow to show that it is ripe.

Bananas provide the body with fibre, vitamin C and potassium. These are vitamins and minerals that are essential for growth.

A banana plantation.

Bananas can also be eaten hot. They can be baked in their skin on an open fire, or they can be used as an ingredient in rice dishes, stews and desserts.

"Eating bananas is a simple and cheap way to be healthier. Do not overlook the wonders of nature that grow here in Jamaica." said the Minister outside the plantation.

1 Why does the minister want people to eat more bananas?

_____

2 What are the places where bananas are grown called?

_____

3   How do you know if a banana is ripe?

_____

4   What do bananas provide that the body needs? Name three things.

_____   _____   _____

5   Bananas can be eaten hot. Describe one way to cook with bananas.

_____

Remember ☆ ☆ ☆

You can use a dictionary to find out the meanings of words that you do not know.

2   Circle four words in the article that you do not know the meaning of. Look them up in a dictionary. Write two of the words and what they mean.

_____

_____

ICT opportunity

Use the internet to find a recipe that uses bananas. How long does it take to cook?

Grammar builder

Look and learn

Adverbs tell you more about how or when actions take place.

              verb   adverb

*The dancer **jumped gracefully** through the air before landing perfectly on two feet.*
   verb   adverb

Many adverbs end in the two letters **-ly**. Here are ten more adverbs you may know:

Word box

badly	gently	quietly	wonderfully
beautifully	happily	sadly	
expertly	quickly	slowly	

Did you know that adverbs like these always have at least two syllables? This is because the **-ly** sound adds an extra syllable to the word!

Easy challenge: Choose an adverb from the word box to complete each sentence.

- A giant fish was spotted swimming _____ off the coast of the island.
- The girl sang _____ at the school concert.

Medium challenge: Write a sentence that contains one of the adverbs from the word box on page 110.

_____

_____

_____

Hard challenge: Write a sentence that contains two of the adverbs from the word box on page 110. Do not use any adverbs that you have already used.

_____

_____

_____

Bonus challenge: Write a sentence to describe what is happening in the picture that you drew on page 105 in the "Speaking and listening" lesson. Try to use at least two adverbs. The adverbs do not have to be from the word box on page 110. You can use any adverbs that you know.

_____

_____

_____

Let's write

L👀k and learn
A **journalist** is someone who writes or reads news items for a newspaper, magazine, TV or radio.

A **witness** is someone who sees an event happening.

1. Work with a partner to write about an event. Choose a different event each time.
   - An old lady stops a thief from getting away.
   - A school raises money for charity.
   - An alien spaceship lands in your town.

Instructions
- You are the journalist of the event you chose. Your partner will be the witness.
- The journalist asks the witness questions. Make notes about the witness' answers during the interview. The witness must answer the questions and describe what happened to the journalist.

Remember ☆☆☆
Journalists need to find out the **five Ws**: **what** happened, to **whom** it happened, **when** and **where** it happened and **why** or how it happened.

2. Write down five questions that you will ask the witness.

_____

_____

112

_____

_____

_____

3 Prepare to write a draft report. Use the notes you made to plan the report. Do not forget to include a headline. Use adverbs to add details to your report.

_____

_____

_____

_____

Editor's checklist box ✓

- Punctuation is important. Look for capital letters and full stops.
- Have you used adverbs?

4 Use a computer to type up your report. You could use columns or include a picture.

Chapter 11

Speaking and listening

1. Listen to to your teacher read the story. Follow the story with these pictures.

An unexpected day

Julie left her house in the morning and set off for another boring day at work. She put on her favourite green dress, fixed her hair and picked up her red handbag. She strolled to the bus stop to wait for the bus that would take her to the office in the city. Julie boarded the bus and took her seat. At the next stop, two men and a lady got on the bus. The lady was wearing a brightly coloured hat. As the lady passed by, Julie looked up and got a big fright! "Christina?" she asked. "Julie?" came the reply. Both women gasped with delight and threw their arms around each other in a big embrace. Julie and Christina were old school friends. They had not seen each other for more than a decade. It turned out they worked in buildings next to each other and they never knew!

Julie and Christina got off the bus together and agreed to meet again for dinner at the end of the day. After work, they went to Diners' Delight, where Julie enjoyed a pizza and Christina had a fresh salad. Julie thought it was going to be just another boring day, she never expected a surprise like that!

Remember ★☆☆☆

When you hear a word you do not know, it is useful to find words within words to help you to work out what they mean. Look at the word *handbag*. It contains the words *hand* and *bag*. So, it must be a bag that is small enough to carry in your hands. Try to use this strategy when you come across words that you do not know.

2. Work with a partner. Retell the story of what happened to Julie by following the pictures. Make sure to keep the events in the correct order. Swap and listen to your partner re-tell the story to you.

3. Decide what you think are the four key parts of the story. Write them in the correct order.

Look and learn

The order that things happen in is called the **sequence of events**.

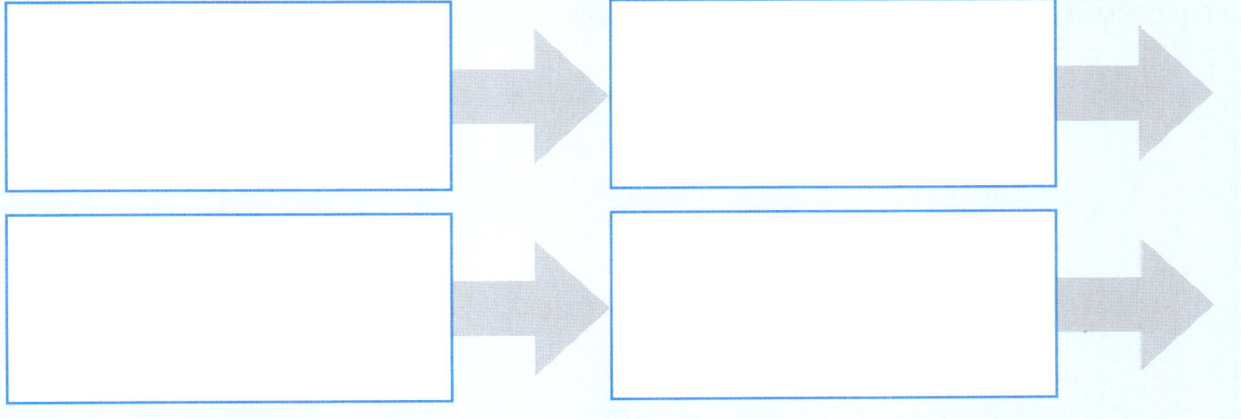

Word builder

Look and learn

Each syllable has a single vowel sound (a, e, i, o, u). For example: **today** = t**o** - d**ay**.

Sometimes the **y** sound has the sounds of **i** or **e**.
- In a one-syllable word, **y** sounds like **i** as in **fly** or **cry**.
- At the end of a two-syllable word, **y** sounds like **e** as in **carry** or **sorry**.
- In a word made of more than one word, like **myself** or **everywhere**, the **y** keeps the same sound as the shorter word.

1 Read the words to a partner. Say each word slowly and count the syllables.

Word box

tiny	finally	myself	shall
better	keep	never	today
carry	puppy	story	everywhere

2 Write the words in the correct columns in the table.

Words with one syllable	Words with two syllables	Words with three syllables

3 Read this passage. Find four of the words from the word box on page 116 and circle them.

This is a story about a dog called Boo. Boo lives with Luke and his family. Boo and Luke are always together. Boo is Luke's best friend. He makes Luke laugh when they play. When Boo was just a tiny puppy, Luke would carry him everywhere, but he is grown now. Luke cannot carry him because he is so big!

4 Write two or three sentences of your own about something that makes you happy. Use words from the word box on page 116 in your sentences.

_____

_____

5 Here are some words from the word box on page 116 again, but something very strange has happened to them. Smiley faces have replaced some of the letters! Write each word correctly. Try to do this without looking at the words in the word box.

Let's read

You are going to read another story about Luke and Boo.

1. Look at the title. What do you think will happen in the story? Talk to a partner.

Boo saves the day!

One Sunday, the phone rang. Luke's mother answered it. It was Luke's aunty. She was very upset because she had lost her new kitten, Tabby. Luke's mom called loudly "Quick, Luke, we are going to help Aunty Sonja!"

"Can I bring Boo?" Luke asked. His mom frowned, "OK, but keep hold of his lead tightly."

They arrived at Sonja's house. "I will check upstairs. Sonja, you look downstairs and Luke, you check the garden carefully", said Luke's mom. Luke ran swiftly into the garden. He was so eager that he let go of Boo's leash. Boo was happily running around the garden when suddenly he stopped. He kept looking into one corner of the garden. "What is it Boo?" Luke asked. Boo put his nose to the ground, as if he was sniffing something. Boo started walking and followed his nose towards the corner. Luke followed. To his surprise, there curled up in the sunshine peacefully sleeping was Tabby. "Good boy, Boo!" Luke exclaimed joyfully. Luke gently picked Tabby up.

> "Mom, Aunty!" he called as he cradled the kitten lovingly. They came rushing outside. "Look! Boo found the kitten. He sniffed it out!" Aunty Sonja was so happy. "Good dog, Boo. You saved the day!"

2 What do you think each character will do next? For example, Luke might give Boo a bone to eat for being such a good dog.

Character	What I think they will do next
Luke	
Luke's mom	
Auntie Sonja	
Boo	
Tabby	

3 Make a list of all the adverbs you can find in the story. There are ten in total for you to find. The first one is written for you.

Remember

Adverbs describe verbs. Most adverbs end in **-ly**.

1. <u>loudly</u>
2. _____
3. _____
4. _____
5. _____
6. _____
7. _____
8. _____
9. _____
10. _____

Grammar builder

Pronouns

1. Read these sentences. Tick (✓) the one in each pair that you think sounds better.

The jam was tasty; the jam was strawberry flavour and the jam had big chunks of fruit.	☐
The jam was tasty; it was strawberry flavour and it had big chunks of fruit.	☐
Jada was running on the beach; Jada was wearing a sunhat and Jada had flip-flops on.	☐
Jada was running on the beach; she was wearing a sunhat and she had flip-flops on.	☐

Talk to a partner about why you think one sentence is better than the other. What is it about the other sentence that is not quite right?

L👀k and learn

Instead of repeating a noun many times in a sentence, you can replace the noun with another word. These words are called **pronouns**. Here are three pronouns:

he   **she**   **it**

There are many types of pronouns.

The words *he*, *she* and *it* are called **personal subject pronouns**. They are also **singular**. This means they refer to just one person or thing.

2 Read these sentences. Find the pronoun that is used in each sentence.

	Pronoun
Martin is a very happy boy because he is always smiling.	
I planted a seedling a month ago and now it has grown very tall.	
My house is very small; it is the smallest house on my street.	
Chris is very good at cricket; he is the star player for the school team.	
Nina's favourite fruit is pineapple; she eats it every day.	

Verbs and subjects

L👀k and learn

Subjects describe one person (singular: *I, you, he, she, it*) or more than one person (plural: *we, you, they*).

Subjects and verbs must agree. If the **subject** describes one person (for example, *he, she, it*), the **verb** usually ends with **-s**.

For example: ***She eats*** *fruit every day.*

3 Read these sentences. Tick (✓) the sentences that are correct and cross (✗) sentences that are incorrect.

	✓ or ✗
He play basketball on Monday.	
She dances gracefully.	
It looks like a beautiful day!	
He leave early to catch the bus.	
She make tasty cakes.	

4 Rewrite the incorrect sentences. Make sure the verb agrees with the subject. Check the endings of verbs carefully.

_____

_____

_____

5 Choose one verb from the word box to complete each sentence. There are three words you do not need.

Word box

jumps   make   likes   want   swims   cooks   play

1 He _____ delicious curry.

2 He _____ in the pool.

3 She _____ on the bed.

4 She _____ to read books about animals.

122

Chapter 11

Let's write

You are going to write a short story about an event that happened in the past. Look back at the story *Boo saves the day!* in the "Let's read" lesson to help you.

1. Copy the graphic organiser in your notebook and complete the sections about your event. You can imagine the story if you wish, but make sure you use adjectives and adverbs to make your story exciting and come alive.

Event / Activity I help my uncle in his garden / planting / digging…
What happened? I found something shiny / hard / in a box / heard a noise…
To whom did it happen?
When?

Where?

Why / How?

2. Discuss your story with a partner. Ask for advice on whether you could add or adjust the details to improve your story.

Remember ☆☆☆

You are writing about something that happened in the past, so your verbs need to be in the past tense.

3. Write your story in your notebook. When you have completed and checked it, show your story to your partner to check it against the editor's checklist below.

Editor's checklist box ✓

Check your work when you finish.
- Did you end every sentence with a full stop?
- Did you include at least three adjectives and adverbs?
- Did you use capital letters for names of people and places?

Chapter 12

Speaking and listening

Origami: the art of folding paper

Here are some instructions to make an origami hat. Work in pairs.

You will need a rectangular sheet of paper that is A4 size or larger.

Read the instructions clearly for your partner to follow. Then swap so that you have both made a hat of your own.

Instructions

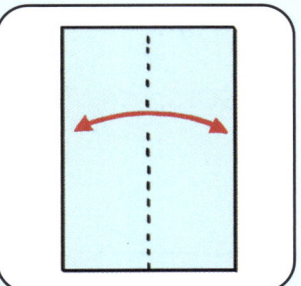
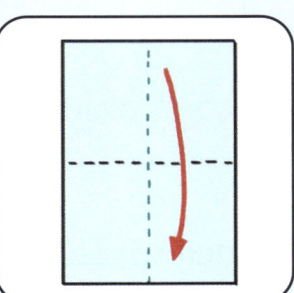

Step 1: Colour one side of the paper and leave the other side blank.

Step 2: Fold the piece of paper in half both ways to make two creases.

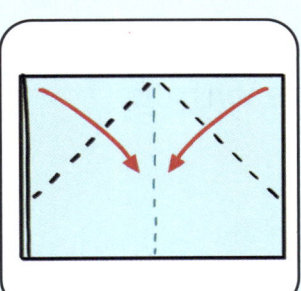

Step 3: Fold the paper exactly in half, so that the colourful side is showing on the outside. Then fold in the top corners so they meet in the middle.

Step 4: Fold the bottom flaps up on each side. Press down to crease well. Now you can open out your hat!

Word builder

Word box

stick	trim	glue	bring
staple	flap	glitter	predict
trace	flip	blobs	plan

1 Read the words aloud to a partner in the style of a robot or computer. Leave one word out of your list. Can your partner find the word you missed?

2 Here are some instructions for making a mandala. Complete the sentences using words from the word box.

You will need: a plate, a pencil, card, paint, glue, scissors, ribbon, glitter.

1 Take the card and use a pencil to _____ around a plate to draw a circle.

2 _____ the card around the circle with the scissors.

3 Decorate the circle with big _____ of paint and allow to dry.

4 _____ shiny glitter all over your mandala with glue.

Look and learn

Look at the word *glitter*. When a vowel (a, e, i, o, u) is followed by an *r*, the vowel changes to a long vowel sound. These are called **r-controlled vowels**.

Say the following words: *cat / car*. Can you hear the long vowel sound when *a* is followed by *r*?

3 Practise saying these words with the vowels *a, e, i, o, u* followed by *r*. Notice that *e, i* and *u* followed by *r* have the same sound = er.

a	e	i	o	u
jar	water	girl	more	turtle

4 Look and say the words. Can you add more words to each box? Look online for more examples of *r*-controlled words.

ar	er	ir	or	ur
car	butter	bird	corn	curl

Let's read

Welcome to Adventure Quest!

You are going to join a quest for adventure! There are 250 levels. Collect lucky beans along the way. Receive superpowers like flying and invisibility. If you are ready for adventure, follow the instructions to create your avatar!

Male or Female?

Choose your clothing:

Select your hair colour:

Add your accessories:

Give your avatar a cool nickname (maximum eight characters):
__ __ __ __ __ __ __ __

Now you are ready to join the quest!

Imagine you are playing the game.

- Create your avatar by following the instructions.
- Draw your avatar in the box. Write the nickname you have chosen and give some facts about your avatar.

Nickname: _____

Level: _____

Superpowers: _____

Lucky beans collected so far: _____

Grammar builder

This term, you have been learning about how to use **adjectives**, **adverbs**, **pronouns** and the **past simple** tense.

Look at this avatar from the *Adventure Quest* game and then read the description of it.

This is Rapid. He has a rainbow of bright colours in his hair. Rapid wears a green track suit to help him run quickly. He wears dark sunglasses to protect him from light beams. Rapid has already collected over a thousand lucky beans and he is only at level 22. He has two superpowers: he can leap so high that he can cross wide rivers, and he can stretch his legs so far that he can reach lucky beans in even the highest places.

1 How many times is the pronoun *he* used in the description? Circle them and count.

2 Find all the adjectives used in the description and circle them. How many are there?

   _____

3 True or false: *There are no adverbs in the description*. If you believe this statement is false, find an example to prove it.

   _____

4 Write your own description of the avatar you created in the "Let's read" lesson. In your description, show that you can use pronouns, adjectives and adverbs.

_____

_____

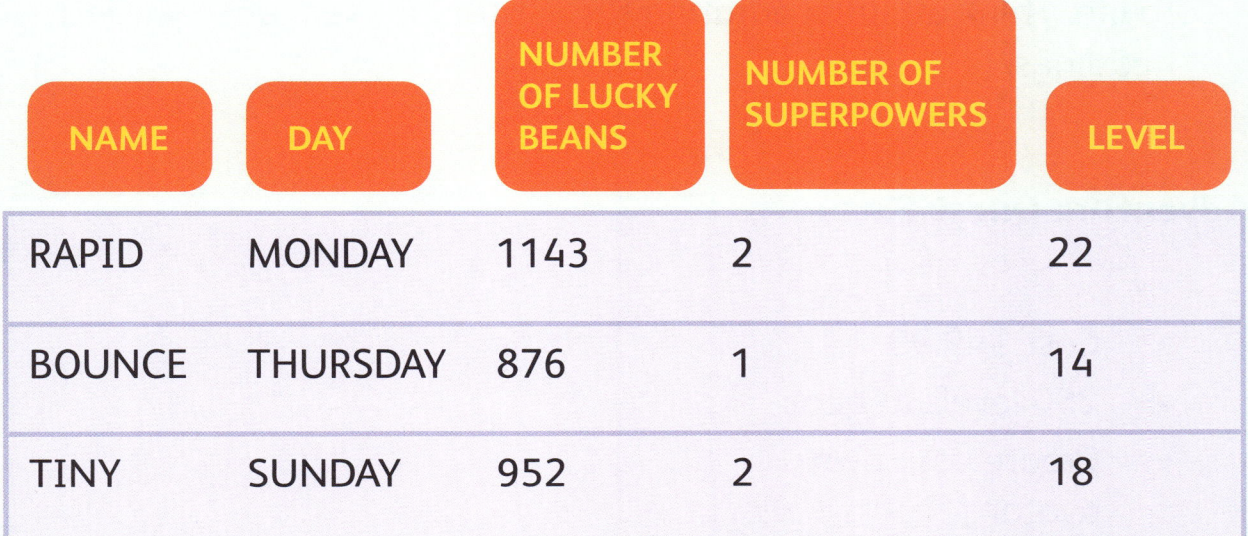

NAME	DAY	NUMBER OF LUCKY BEANS	NUMBER OF SUPERPOWERS	LEVEL
RAPID	MONDAY	1143	2	22
BOUNCE	THURSDAY	876	1	14
TINY	SUNDAY	952	2	18

Rapid played *Adventure Quest* on Monday. He made it to level 22 and he collected 1143 lucky beans. He won two superpowers.

5 Choose either Bounce or Tiny. Write about what happened when they last played *Adventure Quest*. Remember to use the past tense.

_____

_____

_____

Let's write

1. Imagine that you work for the company that makes *Adventure Quest*. Design a poster to promote the game. You are given some facts below to use on your poster. Choose the most important ones to go on your poster.

   Your poster needs to be exciting and attractive. Use lots of adjectives and adverbs to give details and to bring the game to life. Think about separating the poster into sections by using headings.

Adventure Quest Facts

- Cost $49.99
- 250 levels to beat
- Create your own avatar
- Collect lucky beans to trade with other players
- Win superpowers
- Team up with other players to defeat aliens
- Suitable for ages five and over

Term 1 Unit 2 Review and assessment

Speaking and listening

1. With your partner, talk about the news you have from your family. For example:

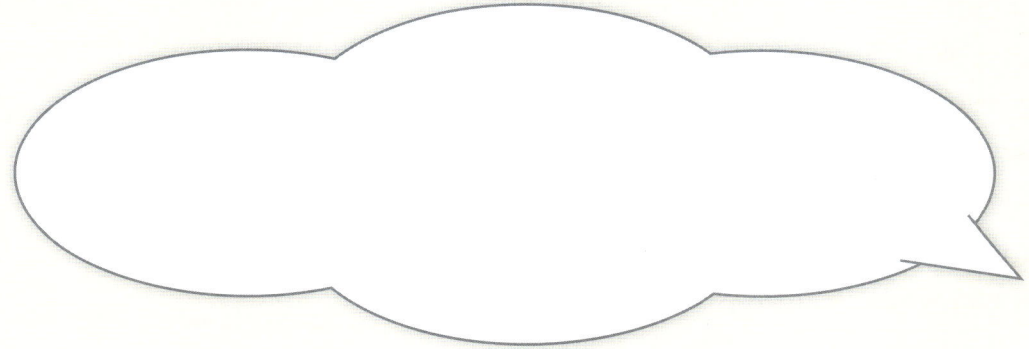

Insert a few notes in the cloud before speaking to your partner.

Word builder

1. Write the words from the word box below in the correct group in the table on page 134.

Word box

skeleton	flew	prize	slow
jewel	bracelet	minister	believe
stain	provide	happy	description
flower	banana	rapid	sunglasses

133

Words with one syllable	Words with two syllables	Words with three syllables

 Let's read

1 Read the newspaper article and answer the questions that follow.

A treat for the whole family

Jamaica's National Pantomime opens on Boxing Day every year and is a treat for the whole family. This year is no different. From the very opening number to curtain close, the audience enjoyed the great music and dance.

The actors surpassed themselves, delivering line after funny line which had the audience laughing. The most enjoyable part of the production had to be the fantastic moving prop that was brought on stage after intermission. No one thought things could get better after the break, but both adults and children were captivated by its flashing lights and moving parts.

Since 1941, the National Pantomime has been providing wholesome entertainment for the family. If you have not seen one before, this is a good year to start that tradition!

1 When does the National Pantomime open each year?

_____

2 What does the writer mean by it "is a treat for the whole family"?

_____

3 How do you know that the audience enjoyed themselves at the National Pantomime?

   _____

4 What does the word "intermission" from the article mean?

   _____

5 What does the line "this is a good year to start that tradition!" tell you about the writer's feelings for the National Pantomime?

   _____

Grammar builder

1 Circle the adjectives and underline the nouns they describe.
   1 The tall man helped his young son across the road.
   2 The shortest runner finished the race first.
   3 The hardworking student won an award.
   4 Jamie got a red bicycle for his birthday.
   5 The blue bag with the heavy books belongs to my best friend.

Let's write

1 Complete the questions using *When, Who, What, Why, How*. Then complete the short article that follows.

   1 The mayor awarded the gold medal to Usain Bolt.

      _____ was awarded the gold medal?

2   The main race started at 11 a.m. _____ time did the main race start?

3   The tickets to watch the games cost $20. _____ much did the tickets cost?

4   Yohan Blake did not get a medal. _____ did Yohan Blake not get a medal?

5   The women's races were held at 2 p.m. _____ time were the women's races?

Usain Bolt was awarded the gold medal at the National games 2021.

_____

_____

_____

_____

_____

Unit 1

Chapter 13

This term will include learning about our community, safety in the home and things made in Jamaica.

Speaking and listening

1. In pairs, take turns to read the speech to your partner.

Introduction:
Hello everyone. My name is Jacob Dean and I am in Grade 3. Today, I would like to talk to you about why you should vote for me as your class president.

Main body:
First, let me tell you how I can make your days at school the best. I will ask the headmaster for two free hours from 12 o'clock every day; one hour for lunch and the second hour for catching up with studying. This will help the students who need extra help and are too shy to ask questions in front of the class. I will also ask for free after-school piano lessons, which I know many of you are interested in.

Conclusion:
Finally, I would like to thank you for your attention and ask you to vote for me. You will not be sorry.

2 Use the speech above as an example to role play your own speech to your partner. Use your own ideas for why you should be class president in the highlighted parts of the text. Use the notes below and add your own to help you when you are making your speech.

Introduction: Hello / my name is... / grade... / why vote for me?
-
-

Main body: Think of two things that you will do for students.
-
-

Conclusion: Thank students / make a final comment as to why you are the best choice for the job.
-
-

Word builder

1 Read the words aloud to a partner. Listen for the *ar* sound in each word.

Word box

car	garden	park	large
far	farm	dark	bark
start	barn	star	part

2 Find words from the word box to complete each sentence.

1. My Dad has a big, red _____.

2. On Saturdays, we go to the _____ for a picnic.

3. At the _____, there is a large _____ for the animals.

3 1 Choose three words from the word box in Activity 1, but make sure they are different from those in Activity 2. Write a sentence for each word.

_____

_____

_____

2 Swap books with a partner. Carefully check each other's work. Correct any spellings in a different-coloured pen.

3 Read each other's sentences aloud, stressing the word chosen from the word box loudly.

Look and learn

Antonyms are words that have opposite meanings. For example: *I **start** school at 8 a.m. I **finish** school at 2.30 p.m.*

4 1 Write the antonym of these words:

far   large   dark

_____   _____   _____

2 For each antonym, write a sentence using that word.

_____

_____

_____

Let's read

My community

A community is all the people, animals and plants living together in one place. A community can be large or small. Your school is a community. The village, town, or city where you live is a community.

In most communities, people live together happily. There are usually places in a community where people can meet, such as churches, halls, libraries, shopping centres or large outdoor spaces like parks.

Everyone is part of the community and every person is important. Every person should take care of the community. They should look after it and take care of the animals and plants. A community should be a safe and happy place to live.

What's your view?
Does everyone in a community have to be the same?

1 Read the sentences and decide whether they are true (T) or false (F).

1. A community is when people, animals and plants live as one group. _____
2. A community can be big, but not small. _____
3. The village, town, city and even your school can be a community. _____
4. People live together happily in churches. _____
5. People should look after the animals and plants in their community. _____

2 What groups or communities do you belong to?

_____

3 Think about the town, village or city where you live. Where do people meet in your community? List the places below.

church

> **Remember** ☆☆☆
> Use **commas** to separate items in a list.

4 Do you think living in a community is better than living by yourself? Explain why.

_____

_____

Grammar builder

Look at this sentence:

> My community has a library a park a hospital and a school

What is wrong with it? Can you see what is missing? There is no punctuation!

The sentence is missing commas and a full stop. Here it is again with the correct punctuation:

> My community has a library, a park, a hospital and a school.

Remember ☆☆☆

Full stops are always placed at the end of a sentence.
Commas are used to separate items in a list.

1 Correct the punctuation in these sentences.
1. On a sunny day it is nice to walk on the beach
2. I live near to a school a church a park and a bank.
3. I went to the shop and I bought some bread some milk a bag of potatoes a bottle of shampoo and a newspaper
4. My community has a zoo At the zoo you can see birds monkeys reptiles and elephants

Remember

Adverbs describe verbs. Many adverbs end in *-ly*.

2 Insert the correct adverb in each sentence to describe a community.

Word box

happily   friendly   safely

1 In most communities, people live together

   _____.

2 The people in my community are so

   _____.

3 Communities work together to help everyone live

   _____.

Let's write

You are going to write a paragraph about your community.

You should write sentences to describe:
- places in your community where people can meet
- natural places in your community, such as parks or gardens
- animals that you see in your community
- people who you think are important in your community.

Look at the "Let's read" lesson on page 141 for some ideas.

> **Remember** ☆ ☆ ☆
> A **paragraph** usually has at least four sentences.

1. Write a first draft of your paragraph here:

   There are many things to do and see in my community. People can meet...

   _____

   Families and friends can go to beautiful, natural places, such as...

   _____

   You can see many different animals, such as...

   _____

   There are also many people who help the community, such as...

   _____

2. Swap books with a partner. Read your partner's work and edit it. Here are some ideas of what to look for. Add more items of your own to the checklist.

Editor's checklist box ✓

Punctuation
- Do all sentences have a full stop?
- Are lists separated by commas?

Spelling
- Check the spelling of …

Word choices
- Check the meaning of …

3. In your notebook, write a final draft of your paragraph. Follow the advice of your partner.

Are your sentences better this time?

Chapter 14

Speaking and listening

1. Work in pairs. Student A describes the picture using the descriptions in the sentences below. Student B closes their book, listens to their partner's instructions and draws what is described in their notebook.

1. In the middle of the picture there is a big house.
2. The house has a door and four windows.
3. On the roof of the house there is a chimney.
4. In the top right-hand side of the picture there is a big sun.
5. Next to the house, under the sun, there is a small hill.
6. On the hill there is a big apple tree.
7. In front of the hill there is a little girl and a little boy skipping.
8. Next to the boy there is a dog.
9. In front of the house there is a garden path.
10. At the end of the path there is a gate.
11. On the left of the house, in the garden, there is a big pond.
12. There is a small toy boat on the pond.
13. There is long grass all around the pond.
14. At the top left-hand side of the picture there are two clouds.
15. Below the two clouds there are two big birds flying.

2 Now swap roles. This time, Student B should make five changes to the picture. For example, reduce the number of windows from four to two or change the dog to a cat. Student A should listen to the new description and draw the picture in their notebook.

Word builder

1 Read the words aloud to a partner. There is a similar sound in every word. Say them to your partner and check with your teacher that you are correct.

Word box

her	person	shirt	girl
stern	bird	serve	dirt
term	third	germ	perfect

2 1 Write the two pairs of letters that make the similar sounds in each word. Share your answers with your partner. Did you choose the same pairs of letters?

_____ _____

  2 Are there any words in the list that you do not know the meaning of? Discuss them with your partner.

3 1 Choose three words from the word box in Activity 1. Write a sentence for each word.

_____

_____

_____

  2 Swap books with your partner. Carefully check each other's work. Correct any spellings in a different-coloured pen.

  3 Read each other's sentences aloud, stressing the word and its sound loudly.

Term 2 Unit 1

Example:

I have so much dirt on my T-shirt.

4 Look at this picture closely. How many of the words from the word box on page 149 can you find to describe it? Here are two clues to get you started:

1   The boy did not come first or second. He came _____.

2   Oh, look there is a _____ in the tree.

> **Remember** ☆☆☆
>
> If you are not sure what a word means, look it up in a dictionary or use an online tool to help you.

5 In pairs, write as many synonyms as you can for the word *stern*.

_____

Let's read

Pre-reading questions
- What is litter?
- Why is there litter?
- Where do you find litter?

1. Look at this picture of a community called Greenville. What has happened here? Circle five problems and say them aloud. For example: *There is litter everywhere*.

2. How do you think the people who live in Greenville feel? For example: *sad*. Use a dictionary or online tool to find other words (synonyms) that are similar to the word *sad*, but describe slightly different feelings. For example: *upset*.

_____   _____   _____

3. Read a news report about what will happen in the town and complete the following tasks.

Local charity saves town!

Mr Mason, local resident.

People of Greenville are about to see the town improve thanks to a local charity.

The charity will help people fix problems in the town. The charity will pay for 20 new litter bins to be placed around the town. This will mean less rubbish and dog mess on the streets.

The charity will also pay to clean graffiti on the walls and repair broken windows.

Finally, they will look after parks and cut the grass.

One local, Mr Mason, said "We are all so grateful. When my neighbours and I heard about this yesterday, we were so happy. We hugged each other, and we all danced joyfully in the street!"

4   Write the things the charity will pay for by completing the words and phrases.

   1   twenty b ___ ___ ___

   2   clean ___ ___ ___ ___ ___ ___ ___ ___

   3   repair ___ ___ ___ ___ ___ ___ ___

   4   look after ___ ___ ___ ___ ___

5   Write the problems that will be fixed.

   1   less ___ ___ ___ ___ ___ ___ and dog mess

   2   clean walls and repaired ___ ___ ___ ___ ___ ___ ___

   3   parks tidy and grass ___ ___ ___ in parks

6   How do people in Greenville feel now? For example: *happy*. Find other words (synonyms) that are similar to the word *happy*, but describe slightly different feelings. For example: *content*.

   _____   _____   _____

Remember ☆☆☆

A **summary** is a short review of the main events.

7   Work with a partner and take turns to summarise what has happened and will happen in Greenville. Remember you do not have to repeat every word from the text. Look at the information in Activities 1 and 2 on pages 151-152 to help you.

Grammar builder

Look and learn

Subjects and verbs must **agree** with each other. This means if the subject is singular, the verb must be singular. If the subject is plural, the verb must be plural.

The dog barks. → singular subject, singular verb

The dogs bark. → plural subject, plural verb

Now we will look at subject and verb agreement using pronouns.

He walks. — singular subject, singular verb

They walk. — singular subject, singular verb

1 Circle the correct subject in each sentence.
1. I walk / walks to school every day.
2. You play / plays the piano really well.
3. He usually eat / eats sandwiches for lunch every day.
4. She like / likes pizza.
5. It stay / stays in the garden and never runs away.
6. We always travel / travels to Trinidad and Tobago for our holiday.
7. You all sing / sings in the choir so well.
8. They usually come / comes to my house at the weekend.

2 Identify the verb and the subject in the sentences below. The first one is done for you.

	Subject	Verb
She watched TV for an hour last night.	She	watched
They went to the cinema on Monday.		
I took the dog for a walk along the beach.		
We played football in the park on Saturday.		
Daniel stayed in school for detention.		
The flowers bloomed in June.		

3 What tense are all verbs in the sentences?

_____

Notice that when the verb is in the **past** tense, all the subjects have the same form of the verb. For example: *I, you, he, she, it, we, you, they* **watched** *TV for an hour last night.*

4 Below are five sentences with missing verbs. Choose a verb from the word box to complete each sentence. Be careful, you need to change each verb so it is in the past tense!

Word box

try   swim   play   eat   go

1   Last weekend, I _____ at the beach.

2   The children _____ together yesterday.

3   Sally _____ to the market on Tuesday.

4   We _____ all the fruit in the basket.

5   I _____ to finish the chores.

Let's write

You are going to plan and write notes for a speech you will read to your classmates. Your teacher will put you into a small team. One team will write a speech that agrees with the sentence below. The other team will write a speech that disagrees with this sentence.

Communities do not need rules

Instructions

As a team, discuss the sentence. Work together to **write a speech** about why you agree or disagree.

- Share your ideas, **make a list** of points and plan your speech.
- Try to **use some evidence** in your speech. **What happened in Greenville**? What is happening in your own community?
- Work together and divide the work between you. If a team member is shy or needs help, make sure someone in the team supports that student.

Example of teamwork:
- Alia should write the introduction and introduce the team to the audience.
- Josh can write about point 1. Anna and Bob can work together and write about point 2.
- I can summarise and write the conclusion. I will also ask if the audience has any questions.

Important: The speech should convince the audience that your team is right. Your audience needs to believe you. When a student makes an excellent point, the people who are listening can clap to show they agree.

1 Use this space to make notes and plan the speech:

> **Introduction:**
> _____
> _____
>
> **Main body:**
>
> Point 1: _____
> _____
> _____
>
> Point 2: _____
> _____
> _____
>
> **Conclusion:**
> _____
> _____

2 At the end of each team's speech, the other team can ask questions. Listen carefully to the other team. Think of some questions to ask. Write them here.

_____

_____

3 When both teams have given their speeches, everyone who has been listening will vote for the best speech. The team with the most votes wins the debate.

Chapter 15

Speaking and listening

The kitchen can be a dangerous place because it is full of hazards. A hazard is something that could cause harm.

This may look like any family kitchen, but look more closely. What dangers can you see?

1. Circle the dangers in the kitchen.

2. Turn to a partner. Have you circled the same things?

3. How and why could accidents happen in this kitchen? Work with a partner. Take turns to ask and answer questions.

4. Write rules to help to avoid three of the accidents you discussed. Use the phrases *You must not*; *You should not*; *You should*; *Do not*.

> **Example:**
> You must not leave a pan on the cooker unattended and walk away.

Rule 1: _____

Rule 2: _____

Rule 3: _____

5. Read your rules to a partner. Then listen to the rules that your partner has written.

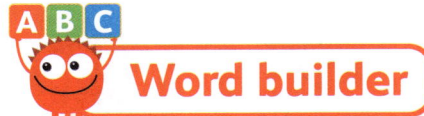
Word builder

1 Here are some words about safety at home. Read the words aloud to a partner slowly. Take care with long words, looking at all the letters and the sounds they make. Use a dictionary or online tool to find the meaning of any words that you do not know.

Word box

hazard	harm	flammable	poisonous
accident	dangerous	electrical	emergency
prevent	safety	sharp	warning

Look and learn

When a word has a double vowel, this is called a **diphthong**. For example: *chair*, *fear*. Note, if the word has a double vowel that is the same letter, for example: *foot* or *feel*, it is not a diphthong.

2 Two of the words from the word box have diphthongs. Write them down.

_____

3 Here are some tips about home safety. Find a word from the word box to complete each tip.

Home Safety Tips

The home can be a _____ place.

Keep _____ knives away from children.

Turn off _____ items when they are not in use.

Read the _____ information on cleaning products.

In an _____ , call an ambulance.

4 All the words in the word box on page 160 have between one and four syllables. Break each word up to show the syllables. Read each word out loud slowly to help you. Ask your teacher to check.

Clapping your hands can help you to find each syllable.

Word	First syllable	Second syllable	Third syllable	Fourth syllable
hazard	haz	ard		
accident				
harm				
dangerous				
warning				
harm				
emergency				
prevent				
flammable				
sharp				
poisonous				
safety				

Let's read

Home safety for the elderly

In Jamaica, there are more old people now than before. This is because people are now healthy and live for longer.

Look around your own home and community. Do you have grandparents or elderly aunts, uncles or neighbours?

Some elderly people need extra special care to help them stay safe at home. When people grow old, their bodies are not as strong. Their bones can become weak. The biggest hazard for the elderly is falling at home. Falls are very dangerous for elderly people because their bones break easily.

Ways you can help the elderly stay safe at home:

- Do not leave rugs or mats on the floor. Old folk can trip over them.
- Have extra handles or bars added to walls and doors for them to hold on to.
- Make sure they always carry their walking stick if they have one.
- Keep everyday items in low places where they can be reached easily.
- Clean up spillages on the floor straight away.

Comprehension

1   Why are there more old people in Jamaica today than in the past?

_____

2   Name some elderly people that you know.
    _____

3   What is the biggest hazard for elderly people, and why is it dangerous for them?
    _____

4   Imagine that an elderly relative was coming to live in your home. What would you say to them to help them feel safe? Share your ideas with a partner.
    _____

5   Draw a picture of one way that you can help old folk to stay safe at home. Write a caption to describe your picture.

Caption: _____

6   Show your picture to a partner. Talk with them about how to keep the elderly safe at home.

Grammar builder

Look and learn

We use the **past simple** to talk about actions that happened in the past.

Regular verbs:
- add **-ed** to the verb:

  I kick**ed** the ball into the goal.
- add **-d** to verbs that end in **-e**:

  I score**d** a goal.
- verbs that end in a consonant **+y**, remove *y* and add **-ied**:

  I stud**ied** for the exams. I carr**ied** all my books home.
- verbs that end in a vowel **+y**, add **-ed**:

  I play**ed** tennis yesterday.

Irregular verbs:

The verb **to be** is irregular. The past simple form is **was / were**.

*My party **was** a surprise. All my friends **were** great and gave me an amazing time.*

1. Complete the dialogue with the correct form of the past simple verb.

   Dan: Hi Joe, I [1]_____ (need) to borrow your History book yesterday. I [2]_____ (try) to call you, but you did not answer.

   Joe: Well, my phone [3]_____ (be) [4]_____ (turn) off because we [5]_____ (be) in the science lab doing an experiment.

Dan: Oh, I see. Well, I ⁶_____ (pick) it up from your desk. I ⁷_____ (look) at your notes.

Joe: OK, but they ⁸_____ (be) for the lesson last week.

Dan: Yes, I know. I ⁹_____ (wish) I ¹⁰_____ (be) in class that day, but I was sick.

2 Write the past simple form -ed, -d, or -ied of the following verbs.

Word box

need _____	study _____
live _____	walk _____
cheat _____	try _____
wish _____	pick _____
play _____	start _____
cook _____	hate _____
enjoy _____	

3 Write the past simple form of the verbs from the word box under the correct pronunciation sound. The first one for each sound is done for you. Sound out the words with your partner and agree on the correct pronunciation. Check your answers with your teacher.

id	d	t
needed	lived	wished

Let's write

> **L👀k and learn**
>
> A **paragraph** has one main idea. This could mean that the paragraph is about one event, place, or time. A paragraph should include:
>
> - A **topic sentence** = main idea. Usually at the beginning of the paragraph.
> - **Supporting sentences** = talk about or explain the topic sentence.
> - **Concluding sentence** = usually the last sentence. It may repeat the main idea or give a final comment on the topic.
>
> When you want to start a new paragraph, you must start the first sentence on a new line.

1. You are going to write a short report titled *Safety first* for a website. The report should have two paragraphs. First, choose one of the titles below for your report:
   - Safety in the kitchen
   - Safety for the elderly

   Then use the structure of the paragraph on page 167 to help you write a first draft in your notebook.

2. Use this space to write some ideas for your report.

> **Topic sentence:** It is important to think about safety in the kitchen.
>
> **Supporting sentences:** Here are three things that people should make sure they do. They should make sure _____ because _____. It is a good idea to _____ because _____. They should always _____, this will help _____.
>
> **Concluding sentence:** If people follow these rules _____.

3. Swap your work with a partner. Ask your partner to read and check your work carefully, then give you feedback. Do the same for your partner.

4. After you have had feedback, write up a final draft of your report. Make any changes you think are needed.

ICT opportunity

You could type out the final version of your report on the computer. Try to use a different style for the title and do not forget to arrange your report into paragraphs. You could also paste in a picture to go with your report.

Term 2 Unit 1

Chapter 16

Speaking and listening

Who makes you feel safe?

1. What job does each person do? Write the name for each job below the pictures.

Word box

teacher   police officer   firefighter
paramedic   nurse

_____   _____   _____

_____   _____

2 In a small group, discuss who makes you feel safe. Share your own experiences and opinions.

    1 What do these people do? Talk about their jobs.

    2 Do you think these jobs are important? Can you say why?

    3 Would you like to do any of these jobs when you are older? Why or why not?

Make some notes about your group's ideas:

3 As a group, give a short speech to the rest of the class about what your group talked about. Each student in the group should say at least one sentence.

> **What's your view?**
> What would happen if we did not have any helpers in our life?

Word builder

1 Here are some words that have to do with community safety. Read the words aloud to a partner. Clap out the number of syllables in each word as you read them. Which two words have four syllables?

Word box

ambulance	police	assistance	equipment
paramedic	hospital	disaster	doctor
firefighter	siren	traffic	rescue

Remember ☆☆☆

A **haiku** is a type of poem that is three lines long. A haiku poem has only 17 syllables in total. The first and third lines have five syllables. The second line has seven syllables. Haiku poems almost never rhyme.

2 1 Use words from the word box to complete each haiku. To help you, look at the first letter of the missing words. Now count the syllables in each line.

Syllables	Fire! Fire!	Accident
five	Fire! Hear the s _____ .	An a _____ came.
seven	Bravely race to the r _____ .	She went to the h _____ .
five	Saving life today.	The d _____ helped her.

2 Write your own haiku using at least two words from the Word box on page 170.

_____

_____

_____

Remember ☆☆☆

A **synonym** is a word that is very similar in meaning to another word.

3 Put the synonyms in the word box under the correct headings in the table.

Word box

| little | slim | swift | big |
| large | fast | tiny | skinny |

small	huge	thin	quick

Let's read

Firefighter Paul has been interviewed by Greenville Radio about his exciting job. Here is how the interview went:

Interviewer:	Morning, Paul. Thank you for joining us today.
Paul:	Good morning. You are welcome.
Interviewer:	How long have you been a firefighter?
Paul:	Almost nine years now.
Interviewer:	Do you enjoy your job?
Paul:	Yes, very much.
Interviewer:	What exactly is your role?
Paul:	I am a driver. This means that I drive the fire truck when we are called to an emergency. Also, I must look after the truck and make sure all the equipment is working.
Interviewer:	Do you drive the truck very fast to get to an emergency?
Paul:	Well, sometimes quite fast, but it is important to stay safe as well. I cannot drive too fast through towns and cities. The siren lets people know I am there so they get out of the way and I can avoid traffic.
Interviewer:	Thanks, Paul. We will hear more from you after this short news break.

1   With your partner, read the interview aloud. Swap over so you both have a turn in each role.

2   Decide whether the sentences are true (T) or false (F). Find evidence from the interview to prove it.

   1   Paul has been a firefighter for over eight years. _____

       Evidence: _____

   2   Paul loves being a firefighter. _____

       Evidence: _____

   3   The most important thing in an emergency is that the

       firefighters drive very fast to get there. _____

       Evidence: _____

Term 2 Unit 1

Grammar builder

Remember ☆☆☆

Proper nouns include the names of people and places. They begin with a capital letter like Kingston, St Mary's School, or Harry. Nouns that are not proper nouns are called **common nouns** like garden, boy or horse.

1. Read the paragraph. Look closely for all the nouns. Circle or underline the different kinds of nouns you find.

Paul lives in the town of Greenville. Paul works as a firefighter. He lives with his wife, Meg. Meg has a bike and she cycles to work as a nurse. Paul's dogs are called Fred and Ginger. Paul goes to work at 7 a.m. and works for eight hours. He has to look after the fire truck and all of the special equipment. When there is a fire or an emergency, firefighters are called to help. Paul's job is to drive the fire truck; it has a loud siren to warn people. Paul has many friends at the fire station like Chris, Laura and Terry, who work with Paul every day.

2. Find at least three nouns from the paragraph to go in each group.

Plural common nouns	
Singular common nouns	
Singular proper nouns	

174

Chapter 16

Look and learn

People and animals are **feminine**, **masculine** or **gender neutral** (neither feminine or masculine). Words for people and animals are feminine, masculine or neuter.

3 Put the words from the word box in the correct group in the table.

Word box

wife	mother	paramedic
husband	brother	doctor
parent	sister	
father	firefighter	

Remember ☆☆☆

Apostrophes show possession, when something belongs to someone or something.

Masculine	Feminine	Neuter

4 Here are some sentences. Rewrite them using an apostrophe. The first one is done for you.

1 The dogs belong to Paul. __Paul's dogs__

2 The bike belongs to Meg. _____

3 The equipment belongs to the fire truck. _____

4 They are friends of Paul. _____

Let's write

The interview with Paul, the firefighter, is about to restart after the news break.

Think of three more questions for Paul and how he would answer them.

Here are some ideas:
- the uniform he wears
- the helmet he uses
- the times of day that he works
- the food he eats to stay strong

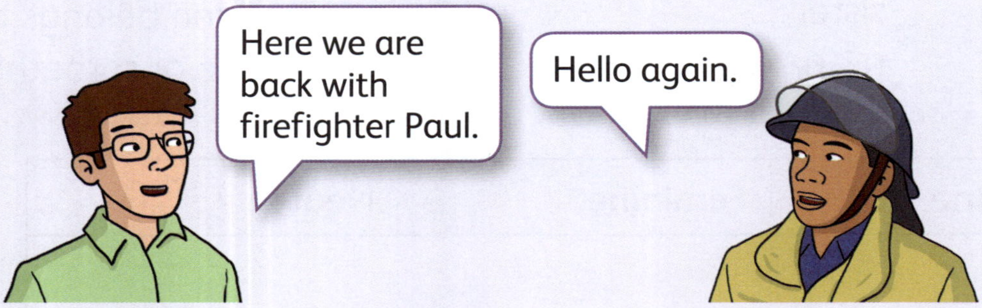

Here we are back with firefighter Paul.

Hello again.

Chapter 17

Speaking and listening

Road safety is important. Crossing a road is dangerous. Road traffic accidents can cause serious harm. Following these simple steps can help save lives when you are crossing the road.

1. In pairs, come up with an action to help you to remember each command. Draw a picture of each action. For example, draw a hand showing that you should stop.

2. Discuss road safety with your partner. What other rules do you know that help you to stay safe near roads? Use the phrases *You must not*; *You should not*; *You should*; *Do not*.

3 Write notes about the rules that you know.

4 Share your rules with the class. Did others come up with similar rules?

Word builder

1 Here are some words to do with staying safe. Read the words aloud to a partner. Listen for the *or* and *ur* sounds in each word.

Word box

torch	report	turn	hurt
horn	more	burn	sure
sore	store	nurse	urgent

2 Choose three words from the Word box. Draw a picture to show the word, then write it underneath.

Look and learn

Homonyms are words that sound the same, but have different meanings. There are two types of homonyms:

- **Homophones** are words that sound the same, but are spelled differently. For example: *to*, *too* and *two*.
- **Homographs** are words that are spelled the same, but have different meanings and could be pronounced differently. For example: *close* (to shut) and *close* (nearby).

3 *Sore* and *saw* are homophones. Complete the sentences with the correct word. Use a dictionary or online tool to check the meaning if you need help.

1 When something hurts it is _____.

2 The past tense of see is _____.

Extra challenge

Find another meaning of the word *saw*.
_____

4 *Store* and *store* are homographs. Use a dictionary to find two different meanings of the word.

1 store:

_____

_____

2 store:

_____

_____

5 Look at the word *sure*. It is a homophone. Find another word that sounds the same, but is spelled differently. Write the other word and what it means.

Word	Meaning

Let's read

Signs all around us

All around you, every day, you can see lots of signs. Signs give you instructions or information, such as directions. They also give you warnings about hazards. Warning signs are used to help people avoid danger. If you follow the advice on a warning sign, you can avoid having an accident or hurting yourself. Signs always use simple words like STOP, so you do not forget what they mean.

1. Think about where you have been this week. Have you seen any signs to help you to avoid danger? What were they? Tell a partner.

2. Here are some signs that you might see in your home, school or community. On each line, write where you think you might see each warning sign.

1

2

3

4

5

3 Write a sentence to describe what you should or should not do when you see each sign. The first one is done for you.

1 <u>You should be careful when you walk on a wet floor.</u>

2 _____

3 _____

4 _____

5 _____

> **L👀k and learn**
> Many **warning signs** have pictures or symbols of the danger.
> Signs often use the colour red as a warning signal.
> Any words used are always short and simple.

4 Look back at the text signs on page 181. Discuss these questions with a partner. Write down your ideas.

1 Why is it important to have warning signs?

_____

_____

2 Why do you think it is important that the words are short?

_____

_____

Grammar builder

A **noun** names a person, place, thing or idea. When something belongs to a single noun the possession is shown by adding an apostrophe and an *s*.

1 Rewrite the sentences using the correct form of the possessive *s*.

Example:
The shirt of the boy was dirty.
The **boy's** shirt was dirty.

1. The punishment of the thief was one year in prison.

   _____

2. The dinner of the dog was eaten by the cat.

   _____

3. The party of the girl was cancelled.

   _____

4. The exams of the school were held in the big hall.

   _____

5. The football of the boy was kicked over the fence.

   _____

2 Look at the information about locations at school. Rewrite the information using possessive *s*.

> **Example:**
> The principle has an office over there.
> The **principal's** office is over there.

1 The school has an Olympic size field.

   _____

2 The hall where we have lunch at school is big.

   _____

3 The room where the teachers work is next to the classes.

   _____

4 The toilet at our school are across from the playground.

   _____

5 The changing rooms at school are next to the sportsground.

   _____

3 Look at the sentences in Activity 2. Make a sign for each that would show people where to go.

> **Example:**
>
> *The Principal's Office*

Let's write

Design a warning sign of your own to help people stay safe.

Remember ☆☆☆

Warning signs must be clear and simple.

Warning signs can contain a picture or symbol of the danger.

1. First, think of some situations that you could give warnings about. Note down your ideas below.

   _____

2. Next, plan the design of your warning sign. Label the different parts.

ICT opportunity

Use a computer to make your sign. Then print it out.

3. In your notebook, write the first draft of a paragraph about how your sign will keep people safe. You should explain what the danger is and the what the sign will do to stop it from happening. Use the text in the "Let's read" lesson and the following paragraph structure to guide you.

> **Topic sentence:** This sign is important because it gives information that is useful.
>
> **Two or three supporting sentences:**
>
> This sign is used to help people _____.
>
> This sign is simple because _____.
>
> **Concluding sentence:** If people follow this sign, they _____.

4. Check your work carefully when you finish. Correct any mistakes and make changes if you need to. Then write a neat final draft.

Chapter 18

Speaking and listening

1. Listen to your teacher read the report about the weather in Jamaica and circle the correct answer to the statements on the next page.

In Jamaica, some people think about things such as politics and sport. However, one of the most common things people talk about in Jamaica is the weather. The weather changes day to day and even from morning to night. In Jamaica, it is very important to know about the weather because dangerous weather, such as hurricanes, can happen when it is sunny or rainy. Hurricanes cause a lot of damage because of their strong winds and they also cause flooding.

The Met Service of Jamaica is the part of the government that watches the weather. They help to make weather forecasts. Weather forecasts tell you what the weather will be like. If a storm is coming, you can prepare and stay safe. Weather forecasts help people in many different jobs, from farmers who are looking after crops to pilots flying aeroplanes out over the ocean.

1. 1 Most people talk about…
      a sport.   b politics.   c the weather.
   2 The weather changes…
      a every day.   b every morning.   c every night.
   3 Hurricanes cause…
      a cold weather.   b sunny weather.   c windy weather.
   4 The weather forecast helps…
      a storms   b weather   c farmers

2. In a small group, read this report out loud. Every student in the group should read part of the report.

3. Discuss these questions with your group.
   1 Why is it important to know about the weather in Jamaica?
   2 What is the Met Service and what do they do?
   3 What do weather forecasts do?
   4 How can weather forecasts help to keep us safe?

4. Share your group's thoughts with the rest of the class. Each student in the group should have a turn at speaking.

Word builder

1. Here are some new words about safety in the country. Read the words aloud to a partner. Use a dictionary or online tool to find out the meaning of words that you or your partner do not know.

Word box

national	people	judge
law	citizens	criminal
prison	security	public
arrest	government	offence

2. Here are some newspaper headlines. A word is missing in each one. Choose a word from the word box to complete each headline. The first one is done for you.

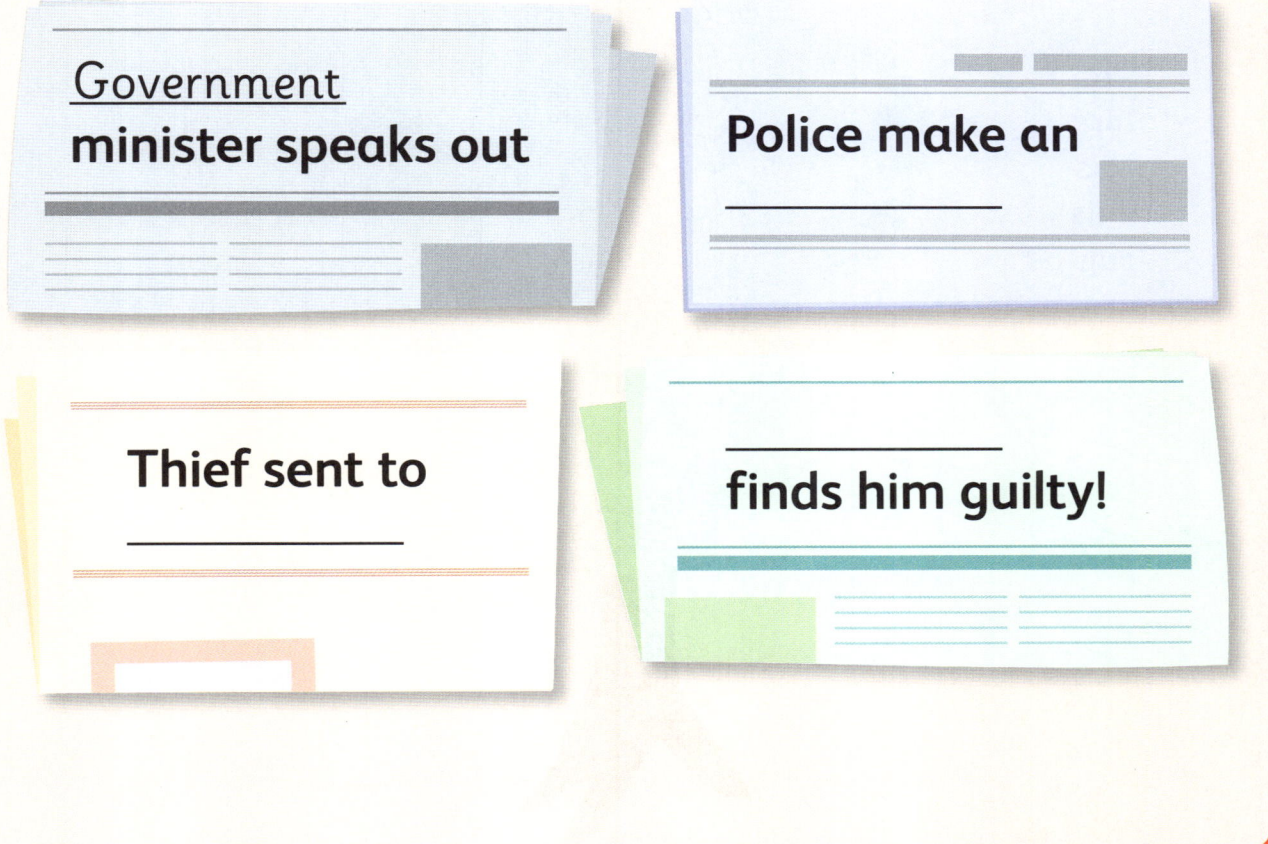

Government minister speaks out

Police make an _____

Thief sent to _____

_____ finds him guilty!

Term 2 Unit 1

Look and learn

- A **prefix** is a part of a word that comes at the **beginning** of a word and changes its meaning.
- A **root word** is the **original meaning** of any word. It is what is left when the prefix and suffix is removed.
- A **suffix** is a part of a word that comes at the **end** and changes the meaning of the word.

3 Look at the picture below. In pairs, make words using prefixes, root words and suffixes in your notebook. Use a dictionary or online tool to help you. Compare your words with other pairs.

Prefixes
(come BEFORE the root word)
For example, re + write = rewrite

re-
pre-
dis-
mis-
un-
en-

Root Words
(Main Word / Base)

write
act
play
tie
agree
read
joy
view

Suffixes
(come AFTER the root word)
For example, write + er = writer

-able
-ful
-ed
-er
-ment
-ly
-ing
-ous
-s
-or

Chapter 18

Let's read

Comprehension

1. Work with a partner. Look at the picture. Predict some answers to the questions.

    1. What are the people doing? I think they are

       _____.

    2. What is their job? I think they

       work for _____.

    3. What kind of music are they

       playing? I think they are

       playing _____.

Look and learn

A **youth club** is a place that has activities for young people.

2. Read the text about the Jamaica Constabulary Force (JCF).

Many people think the police only stop crime, but they do a lot of other activities, too. For example, the JCF have their own band. You can see them playing instruments in the picture. They also have youth clubs for children. At these clubs, children can have music lessons. If children want help with their school homework, they can get this at the youth club. Also, the JCF often visit schools to talk to children about road safety. So, the JCF help all Jamaicans, the young and the old.

3 Answer the questions.

1 Who are the Jamaican Constabulary Force?
_____

2 How are the picture and the text linked?
_____

3 Were you surprised to learn that the JCF have a band? Explain why.
_____
_____

4 List three ways that the JCF help children.
_____
_____

4 Work in a group and discuss the following questions.

1 Why do you think the JCF have youth clubs?
2 Would you like to go to a JCF youth club? Why or why not?
3 Can you think of one thing you can do to help your country? For example, by helping people, being kind to other people, by keeping Jamaica clean.

Chapter 18

 **Grammar builder**

Past participles

Look and learn

We use the **past participle** to change the form of a verb.

Type of verb	Present simple	Past simple	Past participle
regular	play	play**ed**	play**ed**
regular	listen	listen**ed**	listen**ed**
regular	start	start**ed**	start**ed**
irregular	speak	spoke	spoken
irregular	write	wrote	written
irregular	read	read	read

1 Complete the table below. Use a dictionary or online tool if you need help.

Type of verb	Present simple	Past simple	Past participle
regular	jump		
regular	watch		
regular	visit		
irregular	do		
irregular	draw		
irregular	choose		

193

2 Work with a partner. Think of two more regular verbs and two irregular verbs. Complete the table with the present simple, past simple and past participle.

Type of verb	Present simple	Past simple	Past participle
regular			
regular			
irregular			
irregular			

Let's write

Local news

Think about a news story that you have seen, heard or read. You are going to write a paragraph to retell the story in your own words.

1 First, use these boxes to help you organise the facts of your story.

| When? | Who? | Where? | What happened? |

Remember ☆☆☆

A **paragraph** has one main idea. This means that the paragraph is about one event, place or time. A paragraph should include:
- A **topic sentence** = main idea. Usually at the beginning of the paragraph.
- **Supporting sentences** = talk about or explain the topic sentence.
- A **concluding sentence** = usually the last sentence. May repeat the main idea or give a final comment on the topic.

2 Write a first draft of your paragraph. Check for spelling and punctuation with a partner or your teacher.

_____

_____

_____

_____

3 Write a final draft of your paragraph in your notebook or on a piece of paper to display on the classroom wall. Use your best handwriting.

Term 2 Unit 1 Review and assessment

Speaking and listening

1. Work in pairs. Choose an activity to describe to your partner, but do not tell your partner. You must not say any of the words in the phrase. For example: *This is something you have when you are hungry. It has two buns and some meat in between. (eating a burger)* Your partner must guess what it is.

Word box

a boat ride in the sea   swimming at the beach
a picnic in the park   tidying my bedroom

Word builder

1. Write the antonym of each word. Use the words in the word box.

Word box

far   dark   large   dirty

1. light _____
2. near _____
3. small _____
4. clean _____

2. Fill in the gaps by finding the correct words from the word box.

1. I live _____ from my school so my parents have to take me by car.

2. I have to work for my pocket money so when my dad's car is _____, I clean it.

Review and assessment

3   In the winter, it gets _____ around 7 p.m. in the evening.

4   There are many buildings and a _____ shopping centre here because so many people live in this community.

Let's read

1   Read the text and decide whether the sentences are true (T) or false (F).

> A community is not just a few people; it is many people who work together to support and help everyone who is part of the community. A community can be large or small. At a school, that means more than just teachers and students. What would happen if some of the workers at a school community did not go to work?

1   A community is more than one person. _____

2   A community can be big, but not small. _____

3   People that are part of a community support each other. _____

4   A school is a community. _____

5   The workers at a school are not part of the community. _____

Grammar builder

1 Circle the subject of each sentence.
  1 Noah likes local fruits such as banana, pineapple, mangoes and tangerines.
  2 They are happy to go on this field trip to the zoo.
  3 Jake and Lori-Ann are going to perform at the school concert.

2 Add the correct punctuation in these sentences.
  1 my friend joe and bob played football with me
  2 i live near a cinema a shop a park and a church
  3 we went to the market in kingston and we bought some fish some vegetables and some meat

1 You will prepare a speech about why it is important to help your community. Think about keeping the streets and parks tidy / meeting places / supporting each other – children and old people / being happy.

Use this space to make notes and plan your speech:

Introduction: _____

Main body:

Point 1: _____

Point 2: _____

Conclusion: _____

Unit 2

Chapter 19

Speaking and listening

1   Listen to your teacher read aloud the story of Bob Marley and decide whether the sentences below are true (T) or false (F).

> Bob Marley was born on 6 February 1945 and died on 11 May 1981. He was an important Jamaican musician. He made reggae music very popular all over the world. His music told stories of his home. Some songs were about politics like *Get Up, Stand Up*.
>
> Bob Marley's mother was a Jamaican teenager, Cedella Booker, and his father Norvall Marley was from the UK. When he was young, his friends gave him the nickname, "Tuff Gong". He started a musical group, the Wailing Wailers with two friends, Peter Tosh and Bunny Wailer. In 1962, Bob Marley and the Wailing Wailers recorded their first two songs called *Judge Not* and *One Cup of Coffee*.

1   Bob Marley made pop music popular.   _____
2   All his songs were about politics.   _____
3   Two of Bob Marley's friends were Peter
    and Bunny.   _____
4   Bob Marley made his first two records
    with Peter and Bunny.   _____

Lk and learn

Key words or phrases are important to the meaning of a sentence. For example: *Bob Marley was born on 6 February 1945*. The key words/phrases are <u>Bob Marley</u> <u>born</u> <u>1945</u>.

2. With your partner, take turns to read the story aloud. While you are listening, underline the key words and phrases.

3. Look at the key words and phrases you underlined and in your own words, retell the main points leaving out everything that is not important.

4. Report back to the class with your summary and say if you think the summaries you hear include details that are not needed.

ICT opportunity

What else can you learn about Bob Marley? Use the internet to find three new facts about him. Share the facts with your friends.

Word builder

Here are some words about jobs:

Word box

profession	driver	monthly	career
manager	work	editor	farmer
actor	gardener	weekly	baker

1 Read the words in the word box aloud to a partner in the style of someone who is very excited.

Look and learn

Adding a new ending to a word can give it a new meaning

Look at the word *garden*. If we add *-er* to the end it becomes *gardener*, meaning a person who tends gardens.

Many words for jobs people do, end in the letters *-er* or *-or*. The ending is added to another related word, usually a verb. Other examples are *teacher* and *sailor*.

Sometimes, when a word already ends in *-e*, we only add *-r*. For example: *drive* and *driver*.

What's your view?
Look at the jobs in the Word box again. Which job would you most like to do? Which one would you least like to do? Explain why to your partner.

2 Put the words from the word box on page 201 in the correct group for jobs ending in -er or -or. Then add one more word of your own to each group.

Jobs ending in *-or*	Jobs ending in *-er*

Extra challenge

In pairs, write sentences using the verbs *drive*, *farm*, *bake* and their new meaning when the word ends in *-er*. You can use whichever tense (past, present, future) is best. Then compare your sentences with another pair.

Example:

He **works** long hours every day in the workshop. He needs a work**er** to help him.

They want to **build** their own house, but they need a build**er** to help them.

1 _____

2 _____

3 _____

Let's read

1. In pairs, take turns to read the following sentences as quickly as possible:
   1. Can you clean the carpet in your car?
   2. The big, bad bug scared all the baby bats in the bushes.
   3. Shana shivered as she was shocked at the short, sharp shout.
   4. Go and get some green grapes from the greengrocer.
   5. Please put your pens and pencils away and practise the piano.

Look and learn

Notice when words start with the same sound (not just the same letter) and are repeated in a text. This is called an **alliteration**. For example: *cookies, candy* and *cupcakes (c); tea and toast for two (t)*. The sounds are consonants and the words do not have to be next to each other. What is the consonant that is alliterated in *Can you clean the carpet in your car*?

Look and learn

The repetition of similar sounds in two or more words is called **rhyme**. In poetry, these words are usually at the end of a line and help create a certain rhythm. For example: *tree, bee, flea, free* all rhyme because they end with the same sound.

Example of a rhyming pattern: line 1 rhymes with line 2, line 3 rhymes with line 4.

The fat cat
1. There once was a tiny, thin cat,
2. Who wanted to grow really fat.
3. He ate and ate just like his mate,
4. But just could not put on weight.

2. Write your own sentence using alliteration. Now, exchange your sentence with a partner, read each other's sentences and identify the alliterated sound.

   _____

3. Match the rhyming words below. The first one is done for you.

   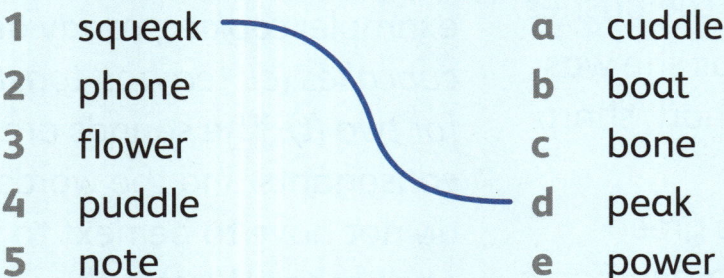

   1 squeak   a cuddle
   2 phone   b boat
   3 flower   c bone
   4 puddle   d peak
   5 note   e power

4. In pairs, read the poem in the "Look and learn" box on page 203 out loud to your partner. Replace some of the words and make your own rhyme. It does not have to make sense, but it must rhyme.

5. Read the following story that can be tricky to say quickly. This is called a "tongue twister". In pairs, take turns to read the tongue twister aloud quickly without making mistakes.

> Betty Bunter bought a bit of butter, but the butter was bitter; if she puts the butter in her batter it will make the batter bitter, but a bit of butter is better than no butter, even if it is bitter.

Grammar builder

An **apostrophe** is a little punctuation mark that has a lot of functions!

> **Remember** ☆ ☆ ☆
>
> One of the functions of an apostrophe is to show possession. **Possession** means when something belongs to someone or something.
>
> The apostrophe is written at the end of the noun and is followed by the letter *s*.
>
> Here are some examples:
>
> *She is Peter**'s** friend.*
>
> *It was Simon**'s** turn.*
>
> *Look at the man**'s** hat!*

> **Remember** ☆ ☆ ☆
>
> To make a noun plural you add *-s*. For example: *There are three boy**s**.*
>
> To show possession, an apostrophe is written at the end of the noun and is followed by the letter *s*. For example: *This is the boy**'s** book.* The apostrophe means that the book belongs to him.

1 Look at these two sentences. How are they different? Discuss with a partner.

I am going to see the boys.

I am going to see the boy's teacher.

2 Choose the correct word from the word box to complete each sentence.

Word box

| kids | dogs | girls | sisters |
| sister's | Mia's | animals | dog's |

1. There are 12 _____ and boys in the class.

2. _____ dinner is cold.

3. Is there any water in the _____ bowl?

4. Where is your _____ bag?

5. I saw so many _____ at the zoo.

6. Look at the mess the _____ have made!

7. Amelia has a brother and two _____.

8. Jayden's Grandad has three _____.

3 Write two sentences of your own. One with a plural *s* and one with a possessive *s* and an apostrophe to show possession. Look at the sentences in Activity 2 to guide you. Compare your sentences with a partner and point out any mistakes you may find.

1. Plural *s*: _____

2. Possessive *s*: _____

Chapter 19

Let's write

Your friend Carla from Cuba has written to you. She told you about her mom's job as a nurse. She has asked what jobs people in your family do.

Choose a job that an adult in your family does. Write a friendly letter to tell Carla about their job. Use the examples in the letter on page 208 to help you.

Here are some things you could write about:
- the name of the job
- the uniform they wear
- where they do their job
- if they enjoy the job.

You should thank Carla for her letter and end the letter in a friendly way.

Editor's checklist box ✓

Check your work carefully when you finish.
- Have you used full stops and capital letters?

207

Address: _____
_____
_____
_____

Date: _____

Dear Carla,

It was so nice to hear from you. Thank you for your letter.
My mom/dad/uncle/aunty is a doctor/nurse/police officer...
_____

The uniform she/he wears is white with...
_____

She/He works in...
_____

My _____ likes/does not like her/his job because...
_____

I hope you enjoyed reading my letter. Please write back soon.
Best wishes,
_____

Chapter 20

Speaking and listening

1. These pictures show two crops that grow in Jamaica. Do you know what they are? Discuss with a partner and write the answer below the picture.

_____   _____

Example:

"I am not sure what it is. It could be ... but perhaps it is..."

"I disagree, I think it is ... because..."

Now, find another pair of students and compare your answers. Use the language in the example to explain the reasons for your answers.

2. Here are another two pictures of the crops above. In pairs, confirm your answers and explain how you know your answer is correct. For example:
This is definitely a ... crop because you can see...

3 Talk to a partner. What other things grow or are made and sold in Jamaica?

<u>tomatoes,   </u>

<u>   </u>

4 Share your ideas with the class. How many different things can the class think of?

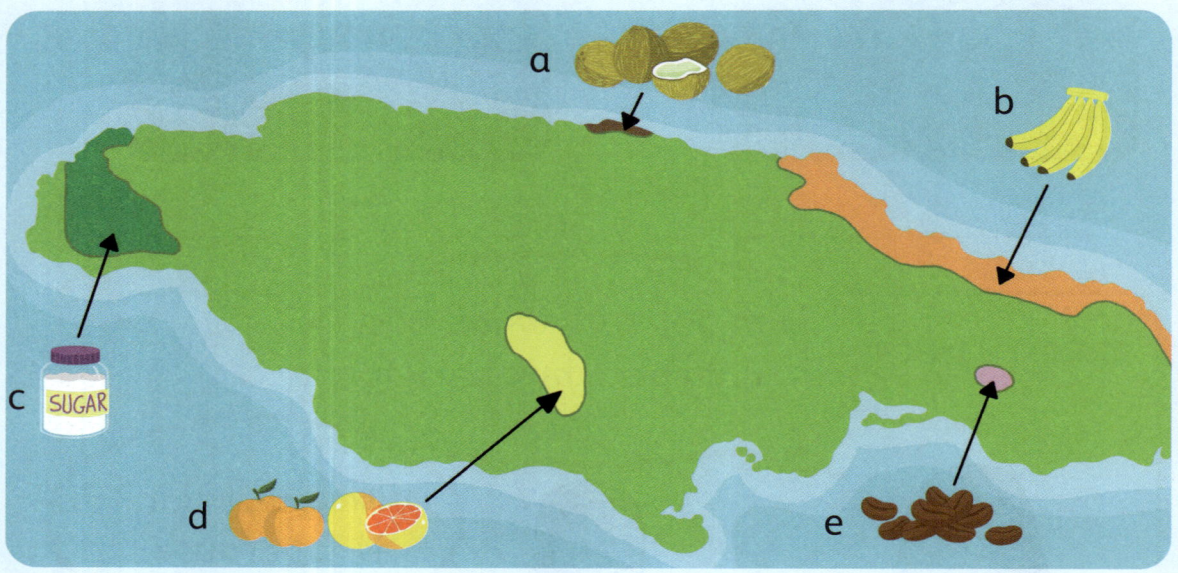

5 Look at the map with a partner. Which crop in Jamaica is your favourite? Which of them do you like the least? Explain why.

6 Choose one crop to discuss with your partner.
- Where does it grow?
- What colour is it?
- How much does it cost you to buy it?
- Have you ever seen or eaten it?

Word builder

Here are some words to do with farming in Jamaica:

Word box

farming	market	coffee	vegetables
plantation	water	harvest	local
crop	coconuts	fruit	agriculture

1 Read each word aloud to a partner. Clap out the syllables to help you.

   1   Which word has the most syllables? _____

   2   How many? _____

   3   How many words have only one syllable? _____

   4   Write them down: _____

2 In pairs, find a word from the word box to complete the sentences.

   1   Today, you can enjoy a wide variety of home-grown

        _____ in Jamaica.

   2   A large area of land that is used for growing a specific

        fruit, such as the banana, is called a _____.

3   When fresh crops are ready, they can be picked, packed and taken to be sold in the shop or at the _____.

4   In Jamaica, Blue Mountain _____ is very popular.

> **Remember** ☆☆☆
>
> **Homonyms** are words that sound the same, but have different meanings. For example: *sore* and *saw*.

3 Use a dictionary or online tool to find two meanings of the word *crop*. Write a sentence for each meaning.

1 _____

2 _____

> **ICT opportunity**
>
> Use a computer to make a presentation about farming in Jamaica. Include some sentences about the crops grown here. Add pictures, too.

Chapter 20

Let's read

Look at the bar graph. It shows how many farmers there are in each parish in Jamaica.

In this bar graph, the tallest bar has the most farmers and the shortest has the least.

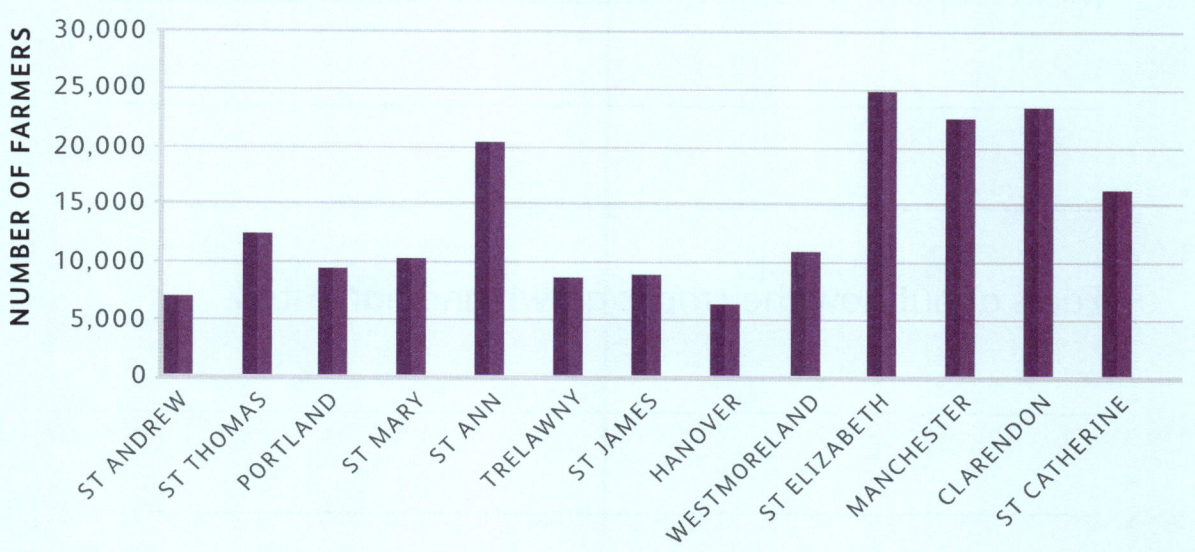

1. 1 Which parish has the most farmers?

   _____

   2 Which parish has the least farmers?

   _____

2. Choose one of the parishes from the bar graph. Do some research about farming in that parish. You can use books, the internet, newspapers or even talk to people for your research. When you finish your research, complete the report on page 214.

Name of parish: _____

Facts about the weather: _____
_____

Main crops farmed (list): _____
_____
_____

Facts about how the crop is grown and harvested:
_____
_____

Facts about where the crop is sold. Where do you buy it?
_____
_____

Facts about how the crop is used. Is it eaten?
_____
_____

Chapter 20

Grammar builder

L👓k and learn

- When you compare **two** things, you use a **comparative adjective**. For example: *The second farmer is **taller** than the first farmer.*

tall   taller

Comparative adjectives often end in *-er*. If the adjective ends in *-y* (*jolly*), swap the *-y* with an *i* and add *-er*. For example: *jolly* ➜ *jollier*.

- What if a third farmer came along who was even taller than the other two? Then you need to use a **superlative** adjective:

tall   taller   tallest

Superlative adjectives often end in *-est*. If the adjective ends in *-y* (*happy*), swap the *-y* with an *i*, then add *-est*. For example: *happy* ➜ *happiest*.

- Some adjectives use the word **more** to make comparisons. These are adjectives that have two or more syllables and do not end in *-y*. For example: *expensive* and *more expensive*. These adjectives use the word **most** for superlatives. For example: *most expensive*.

- Be careful! Some adjectives are irregular! For example:
good, better, best
bad, worse, worst

1 Complete the sentences. Use the correct form of the adjective in brackets.

1 Blue Mountain coffee is the _____ coffee in the Caribbean. (good)

2 Martin thinks bananas are _____ than grapefruits. (tasty)

3 Jackson's plantation is _____ than his neighbour's. (small)

4 The market in Kingston is the _____ in the area. (large)

5 "Mangoes from Jamaica are the _____ I have ever had!" (juicy)

6 Sofia thinks that mountains are _____ than beaches. (beautiful)

2 Look at bullet points in the "Look and learn" box. Write a sentence for each point in your notebook. Compare your work with a partner and check your sentences with your teacher.

Let's write

Work with a partner. Choose one crop that is grown and sold in Jamaica. You may find it useful to look back at your research on farming in parishes in the "Let's read" lesson.

Suggestions: Bananas, coffee, coconuts, citrus fruits, cocoa, sugarcane.

Research the following together. Find out:
- where the food crop comes from
- how it is grown and harvested
- how it gets to the shop or market for you to buy
- what you can do with it.

You can use books, newspapers, magazines or the internet for your research, or you can interview people.

1. In the space on page 218, make a mind map to organise what you find out. Write the name of the crop in the middle and make notes around it.

2. Use your notes to make a presentation. Your presentation can be given like a speech. You can show the class some pictures or you could use the computer to make a slide show.

3. In pairs, give your presentation to the class. Talk for no more than two minutes.

4. Listen to the presentations given by others. Remember to listen carefully, you may find out some very interesting facts!

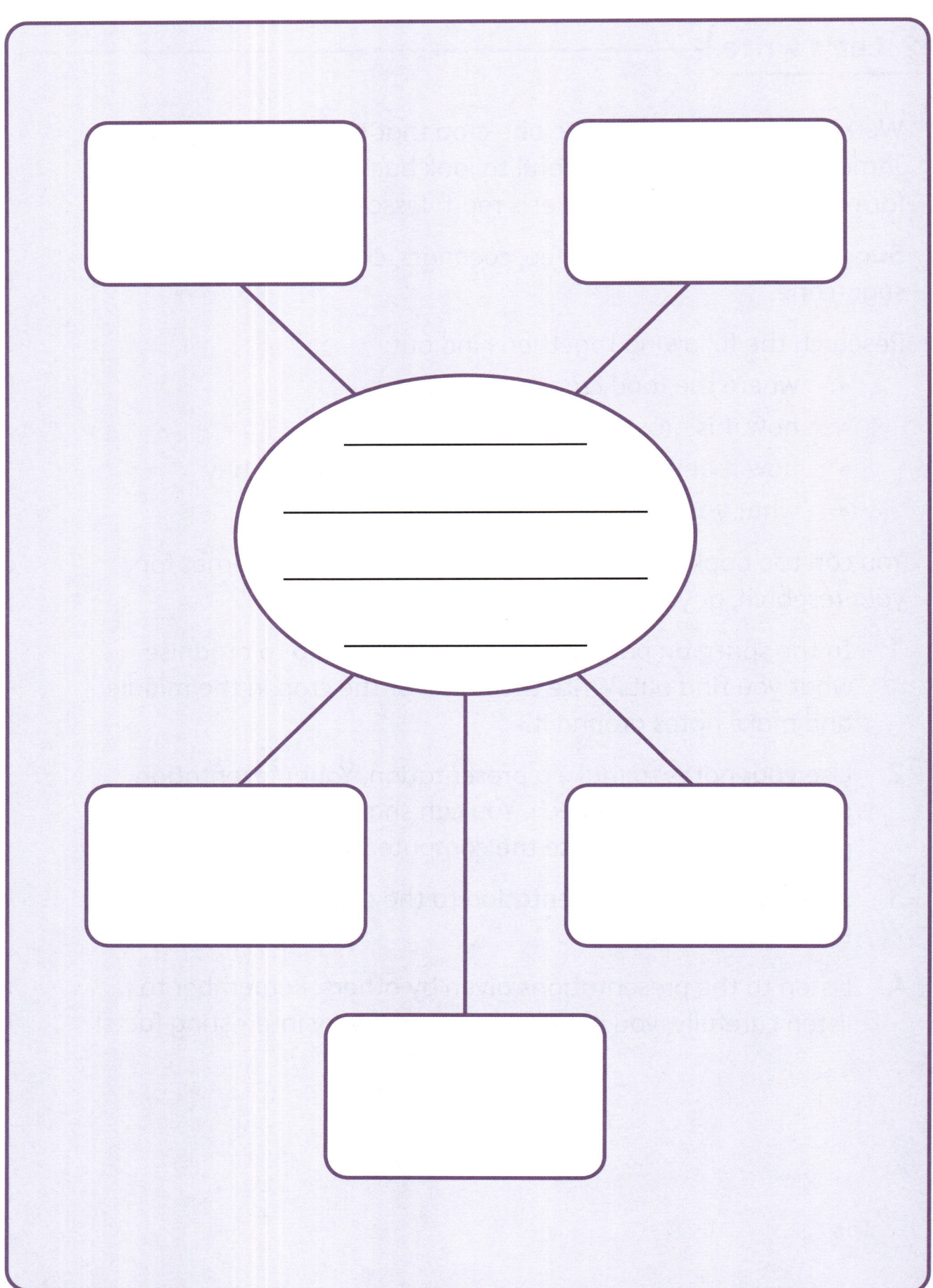

Chapter 21

Speaking and listening

1. Here are advertisements for four products. With your partner, or in a small group, read each advertisement aloud. Emphasise all the good things about each product.

A **Super Clean!**
Get rid of any stain on any carpet or surface with this easy-to-use foam.
Simply spray, wipe and the stain is gone! Available in your local shop,
only $500

B  **Family Treat Box**
All your favourite family treats for a special price of $800!
Contains: 4 Choco Loco bars, 4 Sugar Sweet bars, 12 packets of chips, 6 cans of Cola Crush and 4 cans of Lemon Light.
Something for everyone, grab a treat box before they are gone!

C **TechCo W201**
Upgrade to the latest TechCo cell phone!
New waterproof and shockproof case.
Going to the pool? No worries with the W201!
Dropped your phone? No damage with the W201!
Visit a TechCo shop and speak to us today!

D **Solar Flex Vest**
Stay cool this season with the new Solar Flex vest.
Unique fabric with built in sun protection so you can enjoy the Sun without worry.
Available as a vest, T-shirt or mini-dress.
Prices start at $3500.

2 Write the correct number for the advertisement that matches each product.

Product	Clothing	Food	Technology	Cleaning
Advertisement				

3 With your partner, or in a small group, discuss which advertisement would be most interesting for each person in your family.

> **Example:**
> My dad would like the Solar Flex Vest because he always runs on the beach when the sun is shining.

Chapter 21

Word builder

Here are some words to do with advertisements:

Word box

advertise	internet	packaging	delivery
television	purchase	guarantee	product
postage	cost	offer	service

1. Read the words aloud to a partner in the style of a jolly salesperson. Use a dictionary or online tool to look up the meaning of words that you do not know.

2. Advertisements often use special deals to get people to buy products. Here are some special deals. Can you find a word from the word box to complete each deal?

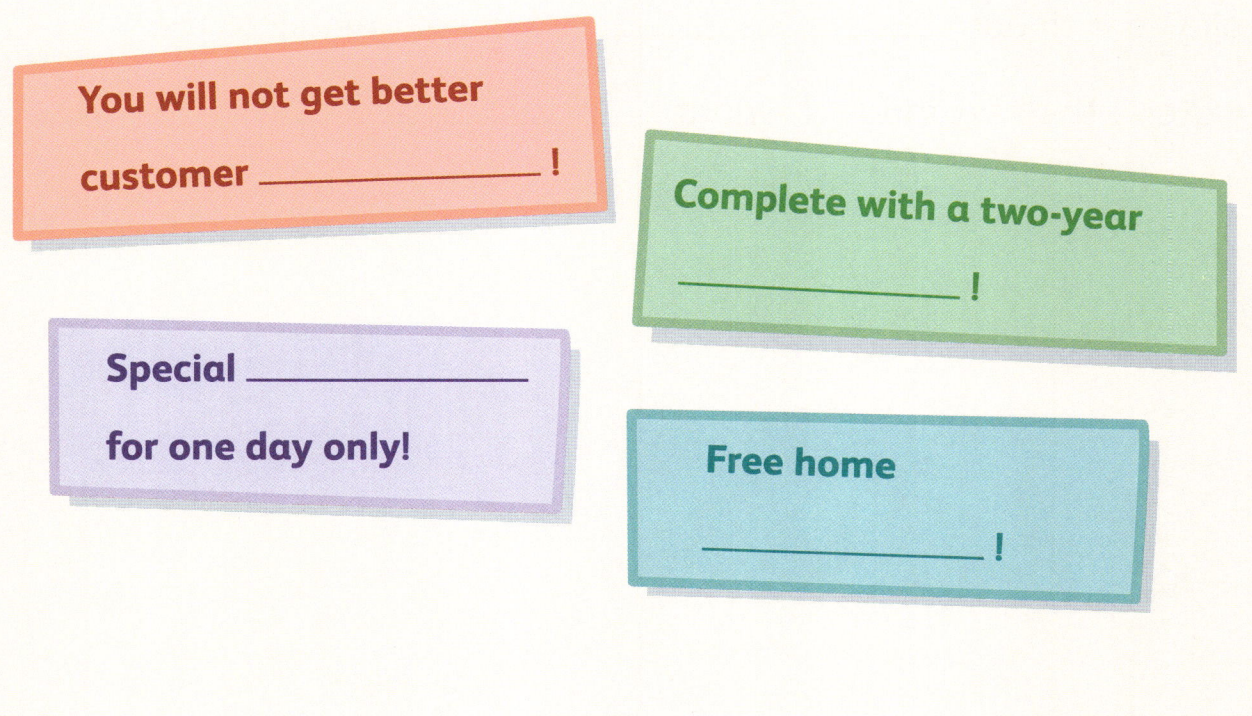

You will not get better customer _____!

Complete with a two-year _____!

Special _____ for one day only!

Free home _____!

Look and learn

Vowel sounds *oy* and *oi* in context

When you hear the *oy* sound at the end of a word or syllable, use *oy* (*boy, toy, enjoy*). When it is at the beginning of, or inside, a word or syllable, use *oi* (*ointment, choice, noise*).

3 Complete the gaps in the text with words from the word box.

Although it rained, we did ¹_____ our trip to the beach. The sand was ²_____ after the rain. We played with our ³_____ instead of going into the water. I think we made the right ⁴_____.

Let's read

1. Advertisements tell us about something that is for sale. They give people reasons to buy it. Here are two advertisements for different brands of orange juice. Read them with a partner.

2. Which of the two advertisements do you prefer? Which brand of orange juice would you buy? Explain why.

   I would buy _____ because _____
   _____.

3. Share what you think with a partner. Did you choose the same brand?

4. Look in some newspapers, magazines, leaflets or on the internet. Find an example of an advertisement that you think is attractive. Cut the advertisement out or print it and bring it to class. Talk to a small group about why you have chosen it.

Grammar builder

Remember ☆☆☆

Conjunctions are words that join together parts of sentences. Four common conjunctions are:

where   when   while   but

Here are some example sentences:

- Joe was listening to the radio **when** he heard the advertisement for the market.
- Joe will go to the market **where** he can buy fruit for a great price.
- Joe wants to go to the market, **but** Lou wants to stay at home.
- Joe will go to the market **while** Lou stays at home.

1 Complete each sentence with a conjunction.

1. I will do my homework in the library _____ it is quiet.

2. Barry was mending the fence _____ it started to rain.

3. Sugar is lovely, _____ too much sugar is bad for you.

4. Mom goes to work _____ the children go to school.

5 The train was late, _____ Paul still went on holiday.

6 It was very windy, _____ the sun was still shining so it was warm.

2 Draw lines to match the two parts of the sentences. You may use each conjunction more than once.

1	Grab a bargain while	a	you need an expert.
2	Shop at TreatMe, where	b	postage is free.
3	Open Monday to Saturday, but	c	stocks last.
4	Call us when	d	prices are always low.
5	Packaging is extra, but	e	closed on Sunday.

Let's write

You are going to create your own crazy invention. Then you will write an advertisement for it!

Choose **one** of these three items:
- a super-tasty, new chocolate bar
- an amazing device to use in the kitchen
- an awesome, new toy or game.

1 Think of a name for your invention. _____

2 Plan an advertisement for it. Here are some things to think about:
- Where will your advertisement be seen? Will it be on paper as a poster or in a newspaper, or will it be on television or radio?
- Do you want to use ICT to create your advertisement?
- Could you record your advertisement on video?

Use the mind map on page 227 to plan your advertisement.

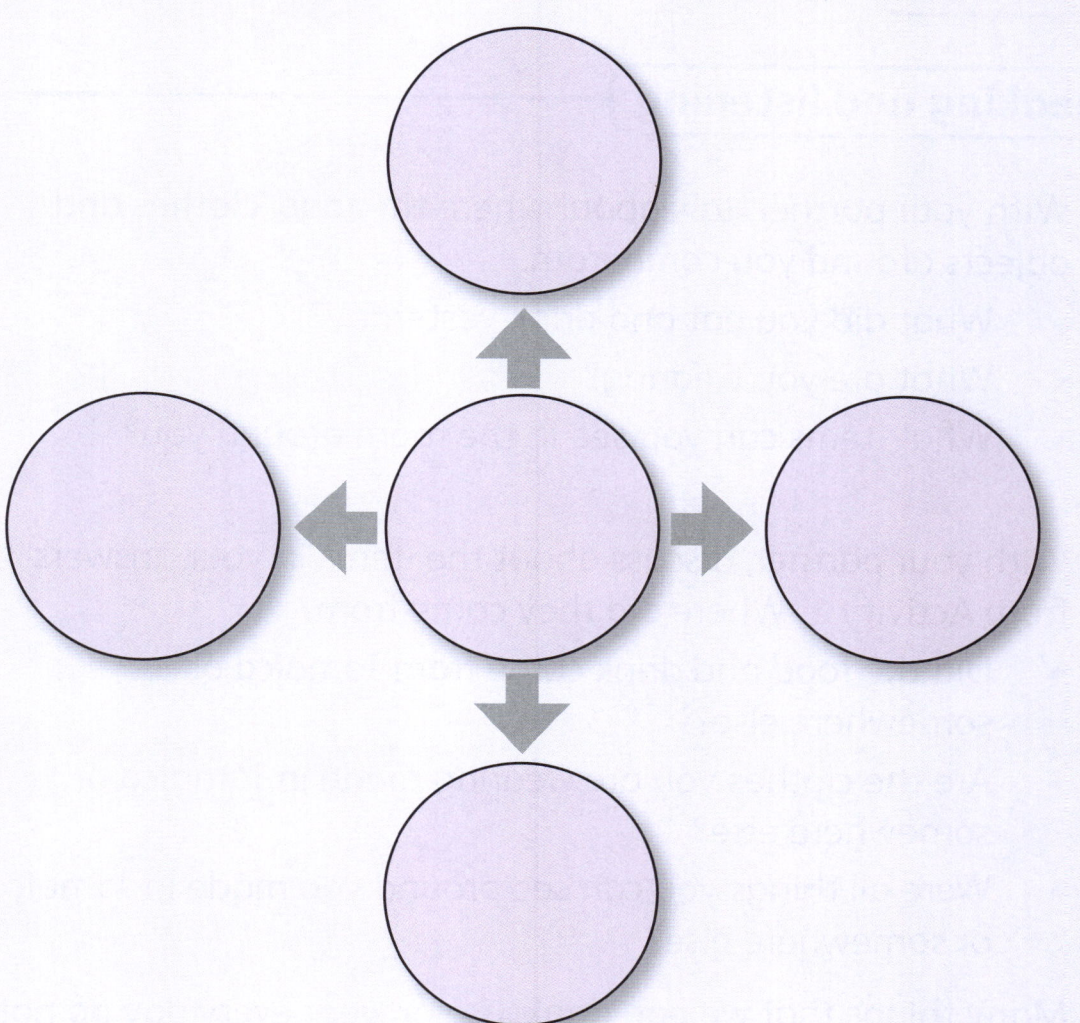

3 Now create a first draft of your advertisement! Remember to check your work carefully and edit it. Use the checklist for editing.

Editor's checklist box ✓
- Think about your word choices. Are they exciting?
- Look at how you organise your advertisement. Is it attractive?

4 Edit your first draft and then do a final version. Share your advertisement with a small group. Talk to them about your advertisement.

Chapter 22

Speaking and listening

1. With your partner, talk about where the food, clothes and objects around you come from.
   - What did you eat and drink yesterday?
   - What are you wearing?
   - What items can you see in the room around you?

2. With your partner, discuss about the items in your answers from Activity 1. Where did they come from?
   - Did the food and drink come from Jamaica or somewhere else?
   - Are the clothes you are wearing made in Jamaica or somewhere else?
   - Were all things you can see around you made in Jamaica or somewhere else?

Many things that we eat, drink, use or wear every day do not come from Jamaica, but from other countries. These items are **imported** into Jamaica. Jamaica also sends things out to other countries. This is called **exporting**.

Chapter 22

3 In the table, list things you have discussed that are made in Jamaica and things that are made in other countries.

Made in Jamaica	Made somewhere else

4 Choose three of the items that were made in another country. Find out what country they were made in.
For example: *iPhone - USA*.

Product			
Country			

Word builder

Here are some words to do with buying and selling:

Word box

import	harbour	ship	south
export	trade	shipping	east
goods	trader	north	west

1 Read the words in the word box with a partner. Decide together whether each word has one or two syllables. Write each word in the correct column in the table.

One-syllable words	Two-syllable words

2 Unscramble the letters to find the words from the word box.

tuhso ☐☐☐☐☐
1

atder ☐☐☐☐☐
2

haorubr ☐☐☐☐☐☐☐
3

haorubr ☐☐☐☐☐
4

pihs ☐☐☐☐
                5

tohrn ☐☐☐☐☐
         6

npgiihsp ☐☐☐☐☐☐☐☐
                    7

Extra challenge

Extra challenge. Write the numbered letters below to reveal the mystery word.

☐☐☐☐☐☐☐
1 2 3 4 5 6 7

L👀k and learn

A **mnemonic** helps us to remember the spelling of difficult words by making up a phrase or sentence where the first letter of each word spells the difficult word you are trying to remember. For example, to spell the word *because* you could say "**B**ig **e**lephants **c**an **a**lways **u**nderstand **s**mall **e**lephants."

3 1 Write a mnemonic phrase for a word about buying and selling from the word box on page 230.

_____

_____

2 Show your mnemonic phrase to a partner, but do not tell them the word. Ask them to work out the word by writing the first letter of each word in their notebook.

Let's read

A **compass** tells us which directions are north, south, east and west. Maps use compass directions to show where countries are.

1. Read the information. Then label the map on the next page.

The Caribbean

The Caribbean region is a group of islands in the Caribbean Sea. To the north and east of the Caribbean is the Atlantic Ocean.

The biggest island in the Caribbean is Cuba. In Cuba, people speak Spanish. Jamaica is south of Cuba. In Jamaica, people speak English and Jamaican Creole.

The next largest island is shared by two nations: Haiti and the Dominican Republic. The flag of Haiti has two colours; blue on the top half and red on the bottom half. There is a picture called a "coat of arms" in the middle of the flag.

Other islands in the Caribbean include Trinidad and Tobago, Dominica and Puerto Rico. The flag of Trinidad and Tobago is red with a diagonal black stripe that has a white line on each side.

Crops, such as bananas and sugarcane from Jamaica, are exported to other Caribbean islands and to other countries all over the world.

1   Write the names of the islands. The first letter has been written for you.

2   Choose two islands. Write the language that is spoken there.

3   What problem might there be if a trader from Jamaica and a trader from Cuba wanted to talk to each other about their goods?

   _____

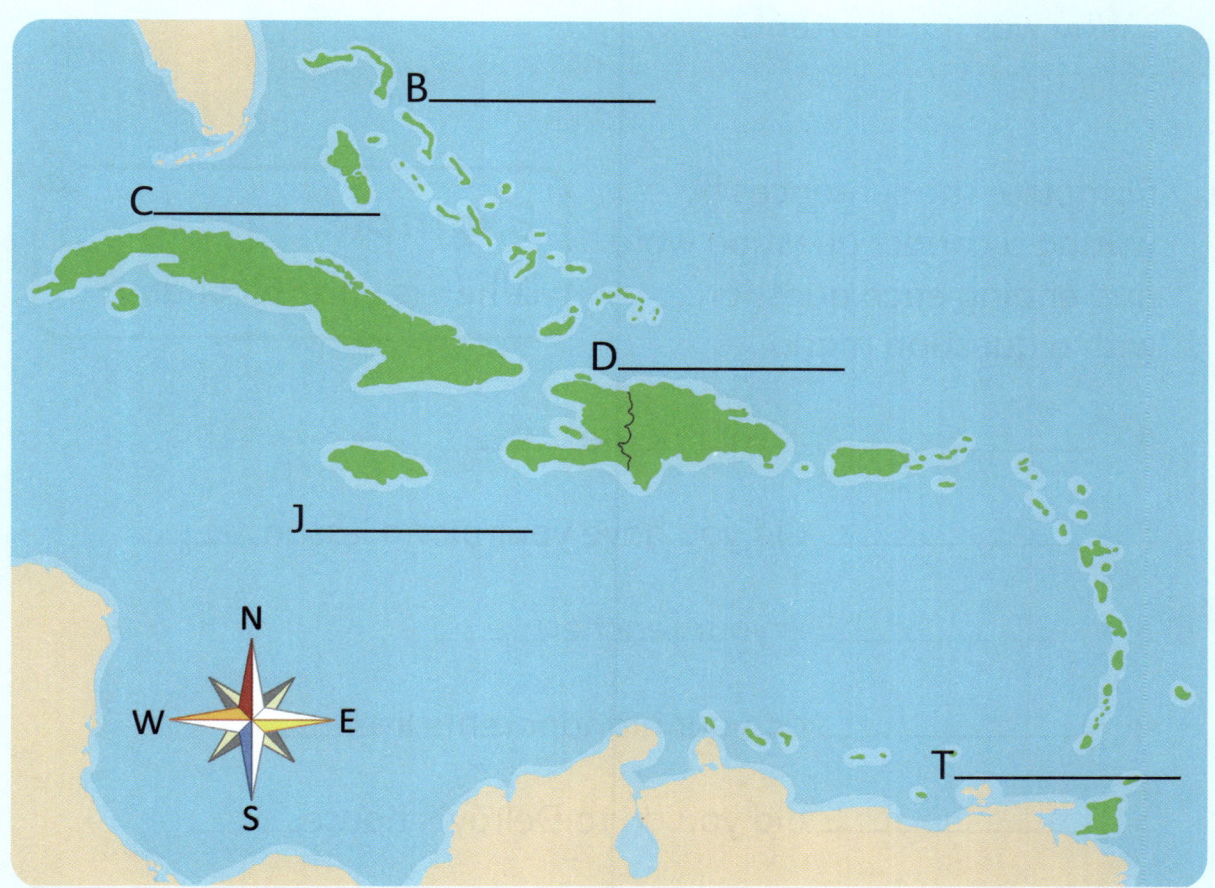

2   Why do you think countries have flags? Discuss your ideas with your partner.

Grammar builder

L👀k and learn

Some words that begin with **wh** are used to ask questions. We often use them to learn about a story or event. For example, we may wish to know:

- Who is it about? / Who was involved?
- What happened?
- When did it happen?
- Where did it take place?
- Why did it happen?
- Why was it important?

1 Complete the sentences by writing a correct question word and ending each question with a question mark.

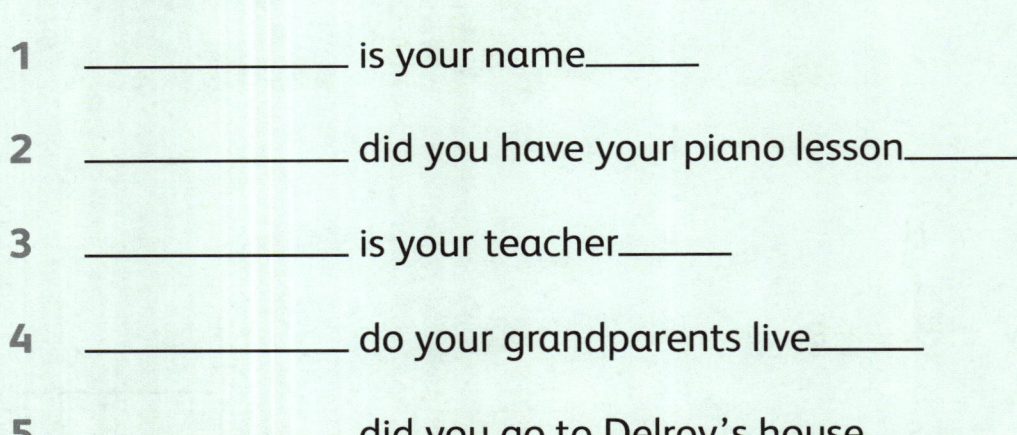

Example:
When is your birthday?

1 _____ is your name _____

2 _____ did you have your piano lesson _____

3 _____ is your teacher _____

4 _____ do your grandparents live _____

5 _____ did you go to Delroy's house _____

2 Read the story below and write a question using each of the *wh* questions in the "Look and learn" box on page 234. Do not forget to end each question with a question mark. The first one is done for you.

> **Bob's family trip to the shops**
>
> Last weekend, I got lost in the shopping centre. My parents, my sister and I were shopping. We went to many different shops and bought clothes, shoes, fruit and vegetables and sweets.
>
> My sister Lucy needed new school shoes. When we were in the shoe shop, I was bored so I started to look at the sports trainers. I thought my sister was trying on the shoes, but when I turned around, I could not see any of my family in the shop. I ran outside the shop, but they were not there.

1 <u>Who went shopping?</u>

2 _____

3 _____

4 _____

5 _____

3 In pairs, swap books and write the answer to each other's questions.

Let's write

Your friend Jake from America has written to you to ask for help with some schoolwork. He wants to know about islands in the Caribbean.

Choose an island in the Caribbean other than Jamaica.
Write a friendly letter to Jake to tell him about the country you have chosen on page 237.
Here are some things you could write about:
- the language they speak
- the flag
- the towns or cities
- what they grow, buy and sell.

You should thank Jake for his letter and close the letter in a friendly way.

Editor's checklist box ✓

Check your work carefully when you finish.
- Have you used full stops and capital letters?

Address: _____

_____

_____

_____

Date: _____

Dear Jake,

_____

_____

_____

_____

_____

_____

Your friend,

_____

Chapter 23

 **Speaking and listening**

Name one thing that is different about you. For example, you are the tallest in the class, you can swim under water for ten seconds or you have ginger-coloured hair.

1. In pairs, take turns to read the poem out loud. Some poems can be sung out loud like a song.

First and Last

I'm the last at school in the morning
and the first out the door at night.
I'm the first one in the lunch queue
and the last to get my maths right.

I'm the last to tidy up after art
but the first in line for P.E.
I'm the last to close my reading book
but first in the playground, that's me!

I'm the last to jump in the water
as we stand at the edge of the pool.
I'm the first to the ice cream van
when it waits outside our school.

I'm the last to complete my story
and to make my writing neat.
I'm the first to leave my table
and stand in line for a treat.

I'm the last to do what I'm told
and to stop my playing about.
But if friends of mine are in trouble
I'll be the first to help them out.

by Brian Moses

Look and learn

The words of a song are called **lyrics**.

Remember ☆ ☆ ☆

Alliteration is when a series of words start with the same consonant sound. Words do not need to be next to each other; other words can appear between them. For example: **B**ill **b**rought the **b**oxes of **b**ananas to the school **b**asement.

2. In pairs, give examples of rhyming from the poem by Brian Moses.

   Rhyming: _____

3. With your partner, discuss what you think this poem means. What message is the poem telling you? Make some notes in the box.

4. Share your ideas with the class.

   What's your view?
   What would life be like if everyone was exactly the same?

Word builder

1 The words in the word box are about how you may feel about yourself or how you feel about others. The blue words refer to nice, pleasant feelings and the red words refer to the opposite feelings.

Word box

wonderful	happy	nervous	angry
cheerful	joyful	annoyed	frightened
excited	bored	disappointed	terrified
surprised	upset	scared	

Write two sentences about yourself or someone you know. Use a word from the blue highlighted words and a word from the red highlighted words. Then check your sentences with your teacher.

1 _____

2 _____

ICT opportunity

Use a computer to type one pleasant feeling and one unpleasant feeling from the Word box. Change the colours and style of the word to show each one feels.

Chapter 23

2 In pairs, select the best word to complete the sentences.

1 Long, longer, longest – The snake is the

_____ animal.

2 Shelf, shelves – There were many books on

the _____.

3 Sharp, sharper, sharpest – This is the

_____ knife in the drawer.

4 Toy, toys – My little brother never puts his

_____ away.

5 Church, churches – My family and I go to

_____ every Sunday.

Let's read

1. Read the poem quietly to yourself. Now, think about the following:
   - What do I understand?
   - How do I connect with the poem: memories, feelings, questions?

Colours

Wouldn't it be terrible? Wouldn't it be sad?

If just one single colour was the colour that we had?

If everything was purple? Or red? Or blue? Or green?

If yellow, pink or orange was all that could be seen?

Can you just imagine how dull the world would be

If just one single colour was all we got to see?

Remember ☆ ☆ ☆

An **antonym** is a word that means the opposite of another word.

2. Look at these adjectives from the poem. Write at least one antonym for each word.

sad: _____

terrible: _____

dull: _____

3   Find and copy two pairs of rhyming words from the poem.

   _____

   _____

> **Look and learn**
>
> **Imagery** is when words and phrases are used to create a picture in the mind of the reader. In other words, imagery sparks your imagination! It can make you use or feel your senses of sight, smell, taste, touch and sound.

4   What can you see in your imagination when you read this poem? Draw pictures.

5   Do you think the poem is only about colours, or is there another message? Talk to a partner.

6   With a partner, read the poem again from the "Speaking and listening" lesson on page 238 and the poem in this lesson on page 242. Discuss the messages in the poems. Is there a connection between them? How are they similar? Share your ideas with the class.

Grammar builder

1 The first line of the poem *Colours* from the "Let's read" lesson contains question marks and apostrophes. Read the information in the "Remember" and "Look and learn" boxes below.

> Wouldn't it be terrible?
> Wouldn't it be sad?

Remember ☆☆☆

You can tell that these sentences are **questions** because of the punctuation. To show when a sentence is a question, you put a special punctuation mark at the end of the sentence. This is called a **question mark**.

L👀k and learn

You have already seen how the **apostrophe** can be used to show possession.

Another way it can be used is to form a **contraction**.

This happens when two words are put together and some of the letters are taken away.

The apostrophe replaces the letters that are taken away.

For example:

Wouldn't is a contraction of *would not*. The apostrophe replaces the letter *o*.

2 Look at the poem *First and Last* in the "Speaking and listening" lesson.

    1 There is one repeated word with contraction. Which one is this?

    _____

    2 Write the full form of the word without an apostrophe.

    _____ _____

3 Write the full form of the words.

    1   I'll   _____ _____

    2   you're   _____ _____

    3   we're   _____ _____

    4   he's   _____ _____

    5   she's   _____ _____

    6   it's   _____ _____

    7   they're   _____ _____

    8   don't   _____ _____

    9   doesn't   _____ _____

    10 didn't   _____ _____

Let's write

There are many different types of poetry. Poems can be long or short. Poems can rhyme or not rhyme.

Across the world, different types of poetry come from different places and cultures, but no matter where you come from, poetry can be read and enjoyed by everybody.

You are going to write your own poem. Your poem will be no more than six lines long and it does not have to rhyme.

First, choose one of these themes. Tick (✓) the one you have chosen.

- working hard ☐
- the Caribbean ☐
- buying and selling ☐
- everyone is different ☐

How to write your poem

Step 1: Brainstorm some words about the theme you have chosen. Try to use imagery by thinking of words that will help the reader imagine a picture in their mind. What verbs will you use?

Step 2: Write a rough draft. You could write a summary of what the poem is about, or you could try out different sentences you would like to use. Check your verbs. What tense will you use?

Step 3: Write out a first draft of your poem. Read it and make any changes to it in a different colour.

Step 4: Write out a final draft of your poem. Check your spelling and punctuation carefully.

Chapter 24

 **Speaking and listening**

Listening is a very important skill. When you listen carefully you will hear more details. You will understand things better. When you listen carefully to another person, it shows that you respect them and that you value what they are saying.

Here is a game to play with your class that involves listening very carefully.

1. Play the game *At the grocer's*, which is all about fruit and vegetables.
    - Sit in a circle. Choose the student who will go first. This student says out loud *At the grocer's, you can see…* and they add the name of a fruit or vegetable beginning with the letter *a*.
    - Then the student on their left says the same sentence out loud, repeats the first student's fruit or vegetable and then adds another that begins with the letter *b*.
    - Continue around the circle, with a new fruit or vegetable being added for each letter of the alphabet.

Look at the picture of the greengrocer shop below to help you to remember the words for fruit and vegetables.

Example:

"At the grocer's you can see an **a**pple."

"At the grocer's you can see an apple and a **b**anana."

"At the grocer's you can see an **a**pple, a **b**anana and a **c**_____."

2   In pairs, ask and answer questions about what your partner's favourite fruit and vegetables are and why they like them. Talk about colour, texture and taste.

Word builder

Here are some words related to poetry, games and songs:

Word box

verse	haiku	memory	feelings
chorus	rhyme	emotion	creativity
syllable	rhythm	imagination	expression

1. Read the words aloud to a partner. Pretend that you are a chef adding the ingredients to a delicious dish!

2. Choose two words from the Word box. Draw pictures or write words or symbols to represent the words. Show them to your partner- can they guess which words you have chosen?

3. Choose two more words from the word box. Make up a mnemonic to help you learn them.

_____

_____

_____

_____

Remember ☆☆☆

A **mnemonic** is a saying that can help you to remember the spelling of a difficult word. For example; **M**y **e**lderly **m**other **o**nly **r**ejects **y**oghurt spells the word *memory*.

Remember ☆☆☆

Synonyms are words that have a close meaning.
For example: *That is a **big** cat. That cat is **large**.*
Antonyms are words that have the opposite meanings.
For example: *I **start** school at 8 a.m.*
*I **finish** school at 2.30 p.m.*

Example:
The **poor** man won a lot of money. He is now **rich**.
(antonym)

4 Complete the sentences by writing the synonym or antonym of the word in italics.

1. It was very *cold* this morning, but now it is _____. (antonym)

2. I like both *large* and _____ dogs. (antonym)

3. I think Maths is *simple* because I find all my lessons really _____. (synonym)

4. When I got Patch from the rescue dog home, he was so *skinny*. Now Patch is too _____ because he eats too much. (antonym)

5. I *love* eating mangos. I _____ them so much I have at least three a day. (synonym)

Let's read

Read this poem by Brian Moses again.

First and Last

I'm the last at school in the morning
and the first out the door at night.
I'm the first one in the lunch queue
and the last to get my maths right.

I'm the last to tidy up after art
but the first in line for P.E.
I'm the last to close my reading book
but first in the playground, that's me!

I'm the last to jump in the water
as we stand at the edge of the pool.
I'm the first to the ice cream van
when it waits outside our school.

I'm the last to complete my story
and to make my writing neat.
I'm the first to leave my table
and stand in line for a treat.

I'm the last to do what I'm told
and to stop my playing about.
But if friends of mine are in trouble
I'll be the first to help them out.

by Brian Moses

L👀k and learn
Poems are broken up into groups of sentences called **stanzas**. They are similar to verses in a song, or paragraphs in a text.

1. How many stanzas does this poem have? _____

2. Find a pair of words in each stanza that rhyme. Write them down.

   _____

   _____

   _____

   _____

   _____

3. Choose your favourite stanza from the poem. Write a sentence explaining why it is your favourite.

   _____

   _____

   _____

Grammar builder

Lk and learn

A sentence is **negative** when it describes something that is not done (or not correct).

Circle the negative sentence:

I will eat my vegetables. or *I will not eat my vegetables.*

Usually, the word *not* is written before the verb in the sentence to make it negative.

Often, especially in speech, the word *not* is used as part of a **contraction**.

I could not eat my vegetables. ➜ *I **couldn't** eat my vegetables.*

1 **Challenge 1:** Convert each of these sentences into a negative sentence.

Challenge 2: In at least three of the negative sentences, use a contraction.

Positive sentence	Negative sentence
The chef will make vegetable soup.	
Granny can go to the market.	
Laurie said he would carry the books.	

The stars were shining brightly.	
The baby was crying.	
Chocolate is healthy.	

Remember ☆☆☆

A **contraction** is when two words are put together and some of the letters are taken away. The apostrophe replaces the letters that are taken away.

2   Write a sentence of your own that is positive. Then write the same sentence and make it negative.

Positive sentence	
Negative sentence	

Let's write

You are going to write a short poem of your own about food.
You could write about food you love or food that you really don't like.
Remember, your poem can rhyme, but it doesn't have to.

1   What food will you write about?

_____

Use the food to spell out the first letter of each line of your poem. Here are two examples. One rhymes and one does not.

JAM

Juicy taste like berries.
And served with bread.
Makes the sweetest sandwiches.

CURRY

Come and discover, you really must try.
Uncover the taste and you'll soon see why.
Rich, hot and spicy, a taste just divine.
Red curry, green curry, Thai curry, too.
Yes, it's many colours, but no curry's blue!

2 Plan a first draft. Spell out the letters on each line.

3 Now write your poem neatly. Check your work carefully. Look at your spellings.

Make the first letter stand out by writing it larger than the others or by using a different colour.

You could type up your poem on the computer and print it out to stick on the wall.

4 Read your poem out loud to the class or to a partner.

Term 2 Unit 2 Review and assessment

1   In pairs, ask and answer questions about what your partner's food is and why they like it. Talk about colour, texture and taste.

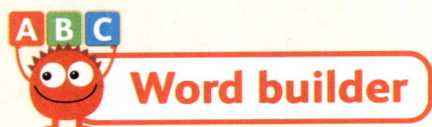

1   Tick (✓) the correct meaning of the underlined word.

   1   A <u>bat</u> rushed out from the cave and frightened us.
       - [ ] a flying mammal that comes out at night
       - [ ] a wooden sporting plank used for hitting a ball

   2   We were told not to play near the <u>well</u>.
       - [ ] feeling healthy
       - [ ] a water source in the ground

   3   The headmaster's office is the second door on the <u>right</u>.
       - [ ] to be correct
       - [ ] the opposite of left

   4   These socks do not <u>match</u>.
       - [ ] a pair of similar things
       - [ ] a stick used to start a flame

   5   What <u>kind</u> of material is it made from?
       - [ ] same as type
       - [ ] the opposite of mean

Review and assessment

Let's read

We are all born
in a different way
How we look
and what we say.

From different countries
around the world
Of different genders:
boys and girls.

Of many sizes
and colours, too
The things we like
and the things we do.

We're sure glad
it works this way.
The world is so colourful
every day.

If everyone were
the same, you see,
You wouldn't be you
and I wouldn't be me!

*by Judith Gorgone,
International Kids Club*

1   Read the poem to yourself. Think about the poem's message.

2   How many stanzas does this poem have? _____

3   Find a pair of words in each stanza that rhyme. Write them down.

_____

_____

_____

4   What is the message of the poem?

_____

_____

Grammar builder

1   Choose the best option to complete each sentence. Use the words in the word box.

Word box

brother's   teacher's   cookies   Tegan's   vegetables

1   There are 15 _____ in the jar.

2   Where is your _____ cap?

3   It's not my bike, it's _____.

4   Who ate all their _____?

5   That's the _____ desk.

Review and assessment

Let's write

Your school is having a concert at the end of the term. Write an advertisement for it.

Here are some things to think about:
- Where will your advertisement be seen? Will it be a poster or in a newspaper, or will it be on television or radio?
- Do you want to use ICT to create your advertisement?
- Could you record your advertisement on video?

Use the mind map to plan the things you need to put in your advertisement.

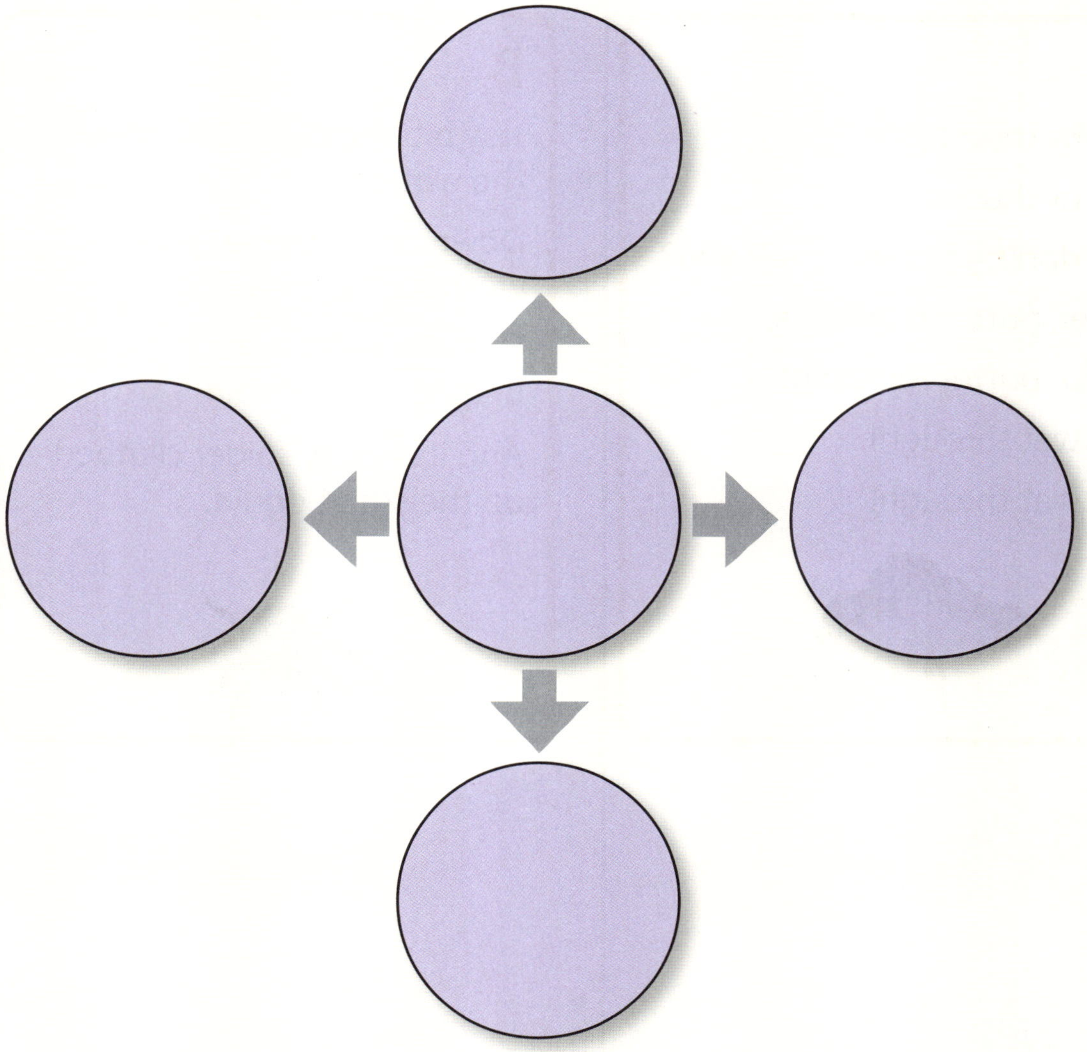

TERM 3

Unit 1

This term will include learning about the differences between non-living and living things, writing a book report and the different languages spoken in the Caribbean.

Chapter 25

Speaking and listening

1. Do you know these rhymes? Work with a partner. Sing them out loud and perform some actions. For example, put your hand behind your ear and say "I hear thunder!".

A

I hear thunder!
I hear thunder!
Oh, don't you? Oh, don't you?
Pitter, patter raindrops,
Pitter, patter raindrops,
I'm wet through!
I'm wet through!

B

Itsy bitsy spider climbed up the waterspout.

Down came the rain and washed the spider out.

Out came the sunshine and dried up all the rain,

And itsy bitsy spider climbed up the spout again.

Chapter 25

2 Both rhymes are about the natural world. One of them is about a living thing and one of them is about non-living things. Write "A" or "B" next to *Living* or *Non-living*.

Living ◯   Non-living ◯

3 What are the differences between living and non-living things? Think about food, water, smiling, etc. Discuss this with a partner. Write your ideas below.

> **Example:**
> Living things need food to grow. Non-living things do not need food because they are not alive.

Word builder

1 Write "L" for living or "NL" for non-living next to the words in the word box.

Word box

apple _____	bag _____	cat _____
ant _____	boy _____	carpet _____
aunty _____	bat _____	car _____
ankle _____	banana _____	comb _____

2 Now make up your own rhyme.

Remember ☆☆☆

The repetition of similar sounds in two or more words is called a **rhyme**. For example: *key, me, knee, sea* all rhyme, because they end with the same sound.

Short poems can follow a pattern in their rhyme.

Example of a rhyming pattern = line 1 rhymes with line 2 and line 3 rhymes with line 4.

The bat under the mat
1 There once was a bat
2 Who slept under a mat.
3 He only woke
4 If you gave him a poke.

ICT opportunity

Use a computer to type lists of living and non-living things. Add as many as you can think of to each list.

To help you plan your rhyme, think of words that rhyme first and then try to join them by writing sentences around them.

> **Example:**
> cat / mat = I have a pet cat
> who sits on a mat.

1 _____

2 _____

3 _____

4 _____

3 **Sight words** are the words that appear often in our reading and writing. In pairs, underline any sight words below you do not understand. Use a dictionary or online tool to look up the meaning.

Word box

about	drink	hot	much	show
better	eight	hurt	myself	six
bring	fall	if	never	small
carry	far	keep	only	start
clean	full	kind	own	today
cut	got	laugh	pick	together
done	grow	light	seven	try
draw	hold	long	shall	warm

Let's read

L👀k and learn

There are two different kinds of writing: **fiction** and **non-fiction**.

Non-fiction writing is about things that are true or that happened, for example, books about history.

Fiction writing is about things that are not true, for example, stories with animals that talk.

1 This is a page from a Science book. Read the page and then answer the questions.

UNIT 4: THE WORLD AROUND US ◀ Heading

Living things and non-living things ◀ Subheading

The natural world is made up of living and non-living things. You are a living thing. The book you are reading is **not** a living thing. The Sun is **not** a living thing.

Only living things grow. Humans grow from babies to adults.

If you look around you, no matter where you are, you will be able to see living and non-living things. Living things can move, eat, have young and grow. Non-living things are not able to do any of these things. ◀ Photo and caption

Mr White's class carried out a survey. They went to three different places and counted the number of living and non-living things they could see, such as animals, plants, people, buildings and cars. **They did not count themselves in the numbers.** Here are the results: ◀ Bold print for emphasis

Location	Living	Non-Living
Park	38	12
Town centre	18	40

◀ Table

Chapter 25

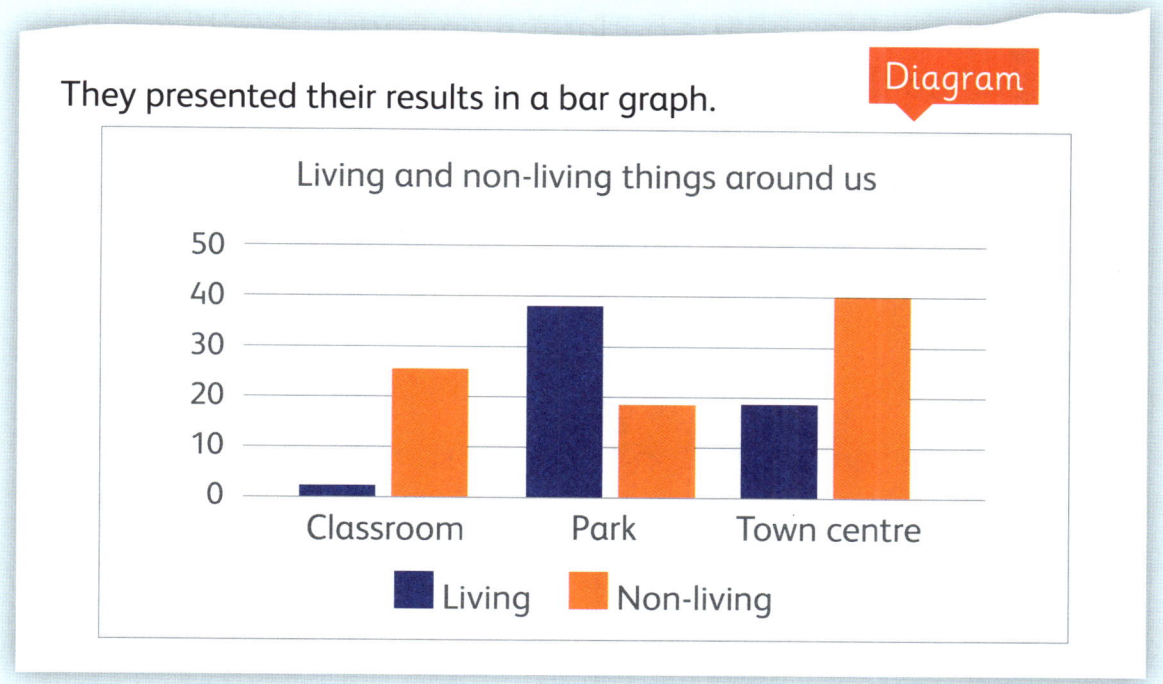

They presented their results in a bar graph.

1   What is the page heading?

   _____

2   What is the subheading?

   _____

3   Why do you think some words are bold in the first paragraph? Discuss them with a partner.

4   Look at the picture of the lady and her baby. What does the picture tell you about the difference between living and non-living things? Use the caption to help you.

   _____

267

2 Look at the table and the bar graph on pages 266-267. Which location had the most living things?

_____

3 Look at the information in the survey. Imagine you are in Mr White's class. For each place, write three nouns for the living and three nouns for the non-living things. Think about people, animals, plants, cars, shops and buildings that you might have seen there. Don't use the same noun twice!

	Park	Town centre
Living		
Non-living		

Extra challenge

Work with a partner. Can you list ten nouns in total for each place?

4 Why do you think there was a difference in the number of living things in the park and town centre? Share your ideas with your partner.

Grammar builder

1. Circle the correct answers. An exclamation mark in writing shows:
   1. strong feelings.
   2. a question is asked.
   3. a statement is made.

> **Remember**
>
> **Statements** end in a full stop.
> **Exclamations** (sentences that show strong feelings) end in an exclamation mark.
> **Questions** end in a question mark.

2. Circle the punctuation mark used for questions.
   1. .   2. !   3. ?

3. Circle the correct answer. A full stop in writing shows:
   1. the end of a sentence.
   2. surprise.
   3. the beginning of a sentence.

4. Write two questions of your own about living and non-living things. For example: *Is a stone living or non-living?*

   Question 1: _____

   Question 2: _____

> **Remember**
>
> There are three main tenses: the **past**, the **present** and the **future**.
> For example: *I smiled, I smile, I will smile.*
> **Non-fiction** texts use the present tense to describe facts.
> A **fiction** text is made up like a story and often uses the past tense to describe the story.

5 Read these two short pieces of writing.

A Some animals live only in water. These animals live in ponds, lakes, rivers, seas and oceans. Small animals, like frogs, live in ponds. Big animals, like whales, live in the ocean. The most common animal that lives in water is the fish. Scientists think there are over 30,000 different species of fish on Earth.

B Timmy, the frog, loved to spend his days splashing about in the pond. He loved to leap from plant to plant, or just lounge in the warm sunshine. One day, Timmy was very hungry when he spied a big, juicy fly. He waited silently for the fly to come within reach. Then, snatch! Timmy's long tongue shot out and snapped up the fly. "Mmm …", said Timmy. "Flies for lunch, my favourite!"

1. One of these texts is fiction and one is non-fiction. Which is which? Write "A" or "B".

   Fiction: ☐

   Non-fiction: ☐

2. Look at the verbs in passage A. What tense are they in?

   _____

3. Look at the verbs in passage B. What tense are they in?

   _____

Let's write

Choose one of the following four topics.

- Animals of Jamaica
- Plants and trees of Jamaica
- Museums in Kingston
- Historic Falmouth

Your task is to write a non-fiction text.
You will write two paragraphs about your chosen topic.
Here is an example:

Heading: *Interesting animals of Jamaica*

Introduction: Animals in Jamaica are very interesting. They include the sea turtle and the patoo.

Paragraph 1: The sea turtle lays its eggs on the coast of Ocho Rios…

Paragraph 2: The patoo has a round face…

Stage 1 – Research your topic.
- You can use newspapers, magazines, the internet or even television or radio for your research.
- Make a mind map or spider diagram of your research notes.
- Find out the facts that you will write about.

- Find some information that you can present in a table or graph.
- Find a photograph to go with your text.

Stage 2 – Write a first draft.
- Decide the main heading. Think about what will be covered in each paragraph. Do the paragraphs need a subheading?
- Begin to make sentences from your research notes.
- Draw a table or graph to go with your text.
- Decide where to put the photograph. Write a caption to go with it.
- Read your first draft. Use the Editor's checklist.

Stage 3 – Create a final draft.
- You can write your text by hand or type it on the computer.
- Don't forget to put in any graphs or photographs.
- Check your final draft carefully. Look out for spelling, punctuation and grammar.
- Display the final draft of your writing on the wall or in your notebook for other students to see.

Editor's checklist box ✓

- Check spellings: look in a dictionary if you need to.
- Check punctuation: have you used full stops and commas?
- Check verbs: non-fiction writing uses the present tense.

Chapter 26

Speaking and listening

There are many games we can play with other people. For example, ball games like *sandy shandy*, musical games where we stand in a ring and sing, or quiet games when we need to think, like *dominoes*.

1 Have you ever played these games or games that are similar? Tick (✓) the games you have played.

2 Work in pairs.

Student A: Explain how to play a game that you enjoy. Think about equipment, the rules, the number of players and how the winner is decided. When you speak, use Standard Jamaican English.

Remember ☆☆☆

Use adjectives and adverbs to make what you say more interesting. For example: I think *hide and seek is a* **fantastic** *game*.

Student B: Listen to your partner explain a game to you. Ask questions about the game to make sure you understand it fully. Use Standard Jamaican English to ask questions.

3 Draw a picture of a game that people play, such as handball, cricket or chess.

You should include labels for the equipment or the items of clothing. You can also include speech bubbles for the players. Think about what they say to each other during the game.

Chapter 26

Word builder

1 Here are some words to do with playing games and sports. Read each word aloud to a partner. Say them in the style of a sports commentator watching a race!

Word box

count	match	play	score
winner	out	player	team
game	pass	point	time

2 1 Write a sentence using each of the words in the table below.
   2 Choose a word from the word box that has not been used to write another sentence.

Remember ☆☆☆

You can make some nouns plural by adding **-s** or **-es** to the end of the word.

game	
point	
team	

275

Term 3 Unit 1

3 These words in the word box below have more than one meaning. Work with a partner. Use a dictionary or an online tool to find the different meanings.

Word box

match   play   pass   point

4 Choose one of the words from the word box above. Write two sentences to show the different meanings.

> **Example:**
> **match:** 1 My shirt and trousers match. They are the same colour. / 2 Let's play tennis and have a tennis match.

1 play: 1 _____ /

2 _____

2 pass: 1 _____ /

2 _____

3 point: 1 _____ /

2 _____

Let's read

1. Skim the text about cricket and tell a partner what the Sabina Park ground is used for. Then read the information more carefully and use a dictionary or online tool to look up any words you don't know.

Cricket crazy

Have you ever seen people playing cricket or have you played in a cricket match?

The game of cricket is one of the most popular sports in Jamaica. The first cricket match was played here in 1895. It is popular with young and old and is played everywhere from small community parks to large cricket grounds.

The biggest cricket ground in Jamaica is Sabina Park in Kingston. Sabina Park can hold just over 6000 people to watch a cricket match. It is also used for other sports including athletics. It has a 400m running track around the cricket pitch.

Sabina Park

Cricket – How is it played?

In a game of cricket, there are two teams of 11 players. A match is divided into parts called *innings*. The teams take turns to bat and to field. A batsman uses a bat to hit a ball that is bowled to him. The other team tries to catch the ball. The batsman runs back and forth between two sets of wooden wickets. The number of runs he gets before the ball is caught, is counted. The winning team is the one that has scored the most runs at the end of the match.

Jamaica has a national cricket team. They play in kit which is the colours of the Jamaican flag; green, yellow and black. They play in matches against other teams from the Caribbean region and from other countries.

> **What's your view?**
> Is cricket more popular than football in Jamaica? Why or why not?

2. Some of the words from the word box in the "Word builder" lesson are in the text about cricket. Find the words and circle them.

3. Are these texts fiction or non-fiction? Explain how you know.

_____

_____

4 Answer the following questions on the text about cricket.

1. When was cricket first played in Jamaica?
   _____

2. What is the name of the largest stadium in Jamaica? Where is it?
   _____

3. How many people does the largest stadium in Jamaica hold?
   _____

4. How many teams take part in a cricket match? How many players are in a team?
   _____

5. How does a team win a cricket match?
   _____

6. What colours are on the kit of the Jamaican national team? Why are these colours used?
   _____

5 How well do you think you are doing with your reading skills? Tick (✓) the box to show how you feel.

☹	😐	👍	☺
I find reading hard.	I find reading hard sometimes.	Good. I'm OK with reading most things.	I'm very confident with reading.
◯	◯	◯	◯

What could you do to improve your reading skills? Think about reading to others or reading a little every day. Talk to a partner. Then share your ideas in a small group.

Grammar builder

1 Rewrite the text with the underlined verbs in the past tense.

I <u>am</u> so happy and delighted. It <u>is</u> my birthday and the party <u>is</u> such fun. I <u>have</u> cakes and a lot of other party food. I <u>have</u> so many gifts. There <u>are</u> a lot of party activities to do. We <u>do</u> not have a bouncy castle but we <u>do</u> have a slide and a small roundabout. Everyone <u>loves</u> the games. Oh, and the best surprise <u>is</u> the clown.

2 In pairs, underline all the verbs. Rewrite this text in the past tense. Compare your text with your partner's.

You run across the road, but a motorbike comes quickly around the corner and nearly knocks you down. You jump on to the side of the road, then leap over a cat. You see your friend, Lucy. She sprints towards you, then you both run towards Lucy's house. You arrive at the door, then ring the doorbell. Lucy's mom opens the door. She shouts "What is happening?" and she tells you to come inside the house.

Let's write

Word box
football   athletics
cricket   basketball

Choose one of the following sports.

Find a book that you can read about the sport you have chosen or about a person who takes part in that sport.

Read the book. Then complete the book report. Colour the stars to give the book a rating.

Book title: _____

Author: _____

Describe what your book is about:

Rate your book:
5 Best book I've ever read.
4 Great book.   2 It was OK.
3 Good book.   1 I didn't enjoy it.

☆ ☆ ☆ ☆ ☆

Explain why you enjoyed it or did not enjoy it:

Editor's checklist box ✓

Check your book report when you finish.
- Have you used capital letters, commas and full stops?
- Have you used adjectives to add details?

Chapter 27

Speaking and listening

1. Listen to your teacher read the texts about folktales. Decide whether the sentences that follow each section are true (T) or false (F).

> A folktale is a story that people have told for many years. In the past, before people had television, books or cell phones, they would sit together in the evenings around a fire. At the fireside, stories were shared. As a tradition, the stories have been passed down through families and many are still shared today.

1. In the past, people had televisions, books or cell phones. _____

2. People today still talk about folktales. _____

> Folktales usually have a moral. This means they have a message or lesson about being a good person or learning from experiences.

3. Folktales are usually about being a good person. _____

> Characters from folktales are well known. One of the most well-known characters from folktales in Jamaica is Anansi.

4. Anansi is a famous character in folktales. _____

> Anansi is a clever creature. He may look like a harmless spider, but he can trick other people and animals to get what he wants. It doesn't always go well for Anansi though. Sometimes he learns important lessons about not being selfish or mean to others.

    5   Anansi is a clever spider. _____

2 In groups of four, read the text on folktales out loud. Every person in the group should read a part of the text.

3 Discuss these questions with your group.
1. Why is it important to share folktales in Jamaica?
2. What lessons can be learned from folktales?
3. Are folktales about real or imaginary life? Give reasons for your answers.
4. What is the most famous folktale in Jamaica?

4 Share your group's thoughts with the rest of the class. Each person in the group should take turn speaking.

ICT opportunity

Use the internet to find another example of a Jamaican folktale. Tell the story to your partner.

Word builder

1 Here are some words to do with stories from our culture.

1. Read the words in the word box below to a partner. Whisper them quietly as if you are telling a story around the fireside.

2. Read the words again. Clap on the syllables of each word, then write the number of syllables next to each word. The first three are done for you.

Word box

folktale __2__	custom _____	legend _____
character __3__	moral _____	ancient _____
tale __1__	fable _____	tradition _____
share _____	story _____	famous _____

Remember ☆☆☆

Synonyms are words with the same or very similar meaning.

2 The words *tale*, *fable*, *folktale*, *story* and *legend* are synonyms.

Look the words up in a dictionary or online tool and decide if this statement is true (T) or false (F).

_____

Look and learn

Sometimes, letters in words are not part of the sound. Letters that we do not say are called **silent letters**. For example, in the word *island*, we do not say the letter *s*. The letter *s* is a silent letter.

3 Look at the words *folktale* and *character*. Say them to a partner. First, sound out each syllable of the word. Then say the whole word. Find the silent letter in each word.

	Silent letter
folktale	
character	

4 Silent letters include *b*, *k* and *l*. Choose one of these letters to complete each of the following words:

ta____k   wa____k   cha____k

thum____   clim____   com____

____nife   ____now   ____nee

Chapter 27

Let's read

1 What words can you think of to describe the Anansi character? Write a word next to each of his boots. Think of adjectives that describe *what he looks like*, for example, *hairy* and adjectives that describe his character or *what he is like*, for example, *clever*.

2 Swap books with a partner. Read the words your partner has used to describe Anansi. How many different words did your partner use? Write them here.

_____

_____

> **Remember** ☆☆☆
>
> **Non-fiction writing** is about facts or things that happened, for example, books about history.
>
> **Fiction writing** is about things that are not true, for example, tales such as *River Mumma and The Golden Table*.

3. Folktales often have animals as characters. The animals can walk and talk just like humans, for example, Anansi the spider.

   Here are the titles of two more well-known folktales. These are not Anansi stories. These are from a group of tales called *Aesop's fables*.

   - *The hare and the tortoise*
   - *The fox and the stork*

   Choose one of the tales to read. Find out what happens in the story. You could go to the library to read the tale, or you could look for a version of the tale on the internet.

4. Talk to a partner. Say what the story about in your own words.

5. With your partner, talk about the moral of the story you read. What lesson did it teach you? For example, it may be about being kind to others.

> **What's your view?**
> Is it important for stories to have a moral? Why? Discuss your ideas with your partner.

Grammar builder

This is a passage from a story called *From Tiger to Anansi*. Read the passage.

> Wednesday came. Anansi made a deep hole in the ground. He made the sides slippery with grease. In the bottom he put some of the bananas that snake loved. Then he hid in the bush beside the road and waited.

1. In most sentences, verbs are doing words or actions.

   Find the words that are verbs in the passage. Circle them.

Remember ☆☆☆

There are three main tenses; **past**, **present** and **future**. For example: *I smiled, I smile, I will smile.*

2. The verbs in the passage are in the past tense.

   Write three examples of verbs in the past from the passage.

   _____

   _____

   _____

3. Use *will* to change the events so they talk about the future.

Example:
Anansi **made** a deep hole in the ground. ➜ Anansi **will make** a deep hole in the ground.

1 Anansi _____ the sides slippery with grease.

2 Anansi _____ some bananas that snake loved in the bottom.

3 Anansi _____ in the bush beside the road and he _____.

Remember ☆☆☆

It is important to check the **endings** of verbs.
The ending must match the person doing the action.
For example: *He **plays** in the yard. They **play** in the yard.*

4 Complete the sentences with the correct form of the verb in brackets.

1 In folktales, the animals _____. (talk)

2 My sister _____ to listen to folktales. (like)

3 We _____ folktales around the fireside. (tell)

4 My Grandma _____ all the old stories. (know)

5 Why don't you both _____ inside and listen to a story? (come)

6 We _____ listening to folktales. (love)

Let's write

1 Choose a folktale that you know. It can be an Anansi story, one of *Aesop's fables* or another tale that you have heard. You are going to work in a group to tell each other stories. You will give a summary of your story to the group. To help you plan your summary, make notes about these things.

Characters

Beginning

Middle

End

Moral

2 Write out your summary neatly.

_____

_____

_____

_____

_____

_____

_____

> **Editor's checklist box** ✓
> - Your final draft should be neat and tidy. Use your best handwriting.
> - Write in complete sentences.
> - Remember to use full stops and commas.

3 Sit in a small group in a circle as if you are at the fireside. Read your summary to your group. Listen to your classmates tell you about the stories they have chosen.

4 As a group, talk about the messages or morals you can learn from the stories. Think about how the stories make you feel and what they make you think about.

Chapter 28

Speaking and listening

> **L👀k and learn**
>
> A **proverb** is a saying. Often, they are warnings, pieces of advice or a wise thought.
>
> For example:
>
> *Early to bed and early to rise, makes you healthy, wealthy and wise.*
>
> This means going to bed and waking up early helps you to be healthy and successful.

1 Here are three proverbs from Jamaican Creole. With your partner, take turns to read them out loud. Put a tick (✓) next to the proverbs that you have heard before.

- Learn fi creep before yuh walk. ☐
- Every mikkle mek a mukkle. ☐
- Trouble nuh set like rain. ☐

2 Work with a partner. Say the English versions of the proverbs. Talk about what they mean.

3 What other proverbs do you know? Write them down. Use an online tool to check you have remembered the proverbs correctly. You may use proverbs from Jamaican Creole or English.

4 Share your proverbs with your partner. Listen to the proverbs your partner tells you. Ask questions about the meaning of each other's proverbs.

Word builder

1 These words are to do with sayings and proverbs. Read the words aloud to a partner. Say them as if you are a wise, elderly person.

Word box

warning	proverbs	truth	meaning
advice	learn	saying	symbolic
phrase	adage	teach	wise

2 Find a word with three syllables from the word box. Use a dictionary or online tool to look up its meaning.

_____

3 This is a short paragraph from a book about proverbs. Fill in the blanks with a word from the word box.

Word box

advice   learn   meaning   proverbs   warning

For many years, people have passed on pieces of

1_____ in the form of 2_____.

Many proverbs are meant as a 3_____ to

stop people from getting into bad habits or behaving badly.

Each proverb has a 4_____ and you can

5_____ from it.

Remember ☆☆☆

When a word ending changes the meaning of the word, this is called an **inflectional ending**.

Look at the sentence: *That is a beautiful painting.*

The word *painting* comes from the root word *paint* with an *-ing* ending added.

Other words we can make with *paint* are: *paint**er**, paint**ed**, paint**s**.*

4

1. Find three words from the first word box on page 295 that end with *-ing*.

2. Write down the root of each word.

3. Write three more words that end in -ing. What are their root words?

4. Look at the Word boxes on page 295 again. Are there any words you don't know the meaning of? Discuss them with your partner. Look them up in the dictionary or using the internet if you are still not sure.

Let's read

1 This is a page from a book about proverbs. Read the page, then answer the questions.

Chapter 6
Farmers and proverbs

English has many proverbs. Lots of proverbs are related to farming. This is because farming is a very old profession. Farmers know so much about the world around them.

- Don't count your chickens before they hatch.
- It's like a needle in a haystack.
- Hold your horses!
- Make hay while the sun shines.

In these proverbs, farming or animals are symbolic of real-life situations:

Don't count your chickens before they hatch.

This means don't rely on something that hasn't happened yet.

Hold your horses!

This means you should slow down.

Like a needle in a haystack.

This means something is going to be very hard to find or a task is going to be very difficult to finish.

Make hay while the sun shines.

This means grab the chance to do something because you may not have that chance again.

1. What is the number of the chapter this page comes from? _____

2. What is the title of the chapter? _____

3. Dayton is always busy. He runs around and sometimes he does so much, he forgets things. What proverb would you say to him? _____

4. Zara woke up early and it was a beautiful day. Her backyard needs tidying. What proverb would you say to her? _____

5. Here are two more proverbs. Choose one of them. What do you think it means?

   - *The early bird catches the worm.*
   - *Stop a while and smell the roses.*

   _____

   _____

Grammar builder

Look and learn

When writing down words that have been spoken by people, you need to use special punctuation marks called **speech marks** or **quotation marks** at the beginning and end of the sentence. A speech mark shows the reader when a person starts and finishes talking. For example:

- "What happened in football practice?"
- "James kicked the ball and scored a goal."
- "Where are the girls?"
- "The girls are playing in the yard."

1. Here is a cell phone conversation between Nina and Anna. Work with a partner. Read the dialogue out loud. Take turns to be each character.

   Anna: "Hey Nina, I have some great news!"
   Nina: "Hi, Anna. Wow! What's up?"
   Anna: "I'm going to the beach today and my mom said you can come, too!"
   Nina: "I would love to come to the beach! Let me check with my mom and I will phone you back."
   Anna: "Cool, speak to you in a minute. Bye!"
   Nina: "I'll be quick. Bye!"

2 1 Use a ruler to underline an example of a sentence with an exclamation mark.

2 Look at the sentence you have chosen. Why does it have an exclamation mark? Write the way the person feels, for example, they may be feeling excited.

They are feeling _____.

3 Nina calls Anna back and says she can go to the beach. Write what both girls say.

4 Swap books with your partner. Check your partner's work carefully. Have they used speech marks and exclamation marks in the right places? Make any corrections in a different colour.

Let's write

Read this story about Adam and his grandfather.

Measure twice, cut once

Adam and his grandfather were cutting wood to repair the fence. They had planks of wood that needed to be cut with a saw. Adam was to measure the wood and mark it, and then Grandfather would cut it.

Adam marked all the planks very quickly. He told Grandfather that he was very good at measuring so they would all be perfect. Adam passed the planks to Grandfather and he cut them exactly in the place where Adam had marked.

Then they took the planks and began to make the fence, but there was a problem. Not all of the planks were the same length!

Adam had rushed his job and some of the measurements were not right. Grandfather said there was an old proverb Adam should know: "Measure twice, cut once!".

1 Write what Adam and his grandfather say to each other when they discovered that the planks were not all the same length.

> **Remember** ☆ ☆ ☆
>
> Make sure to use speech marks. Start a new line each time a new person starts talking.

2 Check your dialogue carefully when you finish. Use the Editor's checklist. Make changes if you need to.

> **Editor's checklist box** ✔
>
> - Have you used speech marks?
> - Have you used full stops and commas?
> - Do questions have a question mark?
> - Have you used exclamation marks to show feelings?

Chapter 29

Speaking and listening

People from the Caribbean share a lot in common, but there are also many differences. For example, in the Caribbean people speak many languages. Here are three children who live in the Caribbean just like you.

Hi, I'm Jodie. I'm from Jamaica.

Hola, soy Jaime. Vivo en Cuba.

Salut! Je m'appelle Christophe. J'habite en Haïti.

1. Talk to a partner. Do you know what language any of the children in the pictures are speaking?

Remember ☆☆☆

Proper nouns are the names of people and places. They start with a capital letter.

2 Even without speaking the language, you can still work out what each child is called and where they are from. Complete the table with their details.

Name	Country

3 Choose one of the children from the pictures on page 303. Do some research about their country. Compare and contrast your daily life with theirs. For example, what is their school like and what do people like to eat where they live? You can use the internet, newspapers, books, magazines or talk to people for your research.

4 Work with a small group. Talk about what you found out. Invite your classmates to ask questions.

> Be sensitive when you ask and answer questions; people and places are different. We must respect other people no matter where they live or what they look like.

5 Talk to your group. Decide if you would prefer to live in the country you talked about or in Jamaica. Explain your choice.

Word builder

1. Read the words in the word box aloud to a partner. As you read, change your tone of voice. Say the first word in a cheery, positive way and the next word in a deep voice, in a negative way.

Word box

culture	traditions	beautiful	dollar
country	tropical	hurricane	coastline
nation	island	modern	proud

2. Draw lines to match the words to their meanings. Start with the words that you already know.

1 modern   The art, writing and languages of a group of people.

2 hurricane   Feeling pleased about something you own or have done.

3 proud   To do with the present, not old.

4 culture   A strong storm with high winds and heavy rain.

Look and learn

Context clues are hints found within sentences or paragraphs that a reader uses to understand the meanings of new or unfamiliar words. For example, *scholar* probably means *a clever student*. The context clue is *As*. A clever student (or scholar) is likely to get A grades.

Example: *He was a good scholar who got straight As.*
                 clever student

3 Read the sentences below. One word in each sentence is highlighted. Choose the word closest in meaning from options a, b or c. (The context clues are underlined.)

1. <u>Tom told his friends</u> he was in the 100 metres race on sports day at school. He ==proposed== that his friends watch him in the race.
   - a asked
   - b predicted
   - c believed

2. The sun was shining, <u>but</u> there were light ==showers== in the forecast.
   - a wind
   - b rain
   - c fog

3. John was ==hesitant== to go to the park <u>because</u> his mom told him <u>dinner was nearly ready</u>.
   - a unwilling
   - b happy
   - c sad

4. John's friends were ==dismayed== by John not going to the park because <u>he said he would</u>, and now they do <u>not</u> have <u>enough people to play football</u>.
   - a upset
   - b OK
   - c happy

5. Betty's friends planned a <u>surprise party</u> for her. She was ==astonished==!
   - a pleased
   - b upset
   - c disappointed

Let's read

L👀k and learn

A **fact** is something that is always true.

An **opinion** is what someone thinks or how they feel about something.

For example: *Ripe bananas are yellow* is a fact. *Bananas are the best fruit* is an opinion.

Opinions can change over time.

For example: *I used to think reading was boring, but now I love it*.

1. In Chapter 26, you decided how you were feeling about your reading skills. What is your opinion now? Has your opinion changed? Tick (✓) the box to show how you feel now.

I find reading hard.	I find reading hard sometimes.	Good. I'm OK with reading most things.	I'm very confident with reading.
◯	◯	◯	◯

Remember ☆☆☆

Non-fiction is about things that are true or happened (facts), for example, books about history.

Fiction is about things that are not true, for example, tales such as *River Mumma and The Golden Table*.

2 Here are some sentences from non-fiction texts. Decide if each sentence is fact or opinion. Tick (✓) the box. The first one is done for you.

	Fact	Opinion
Jamaica is an island in the Caribbean.	✓	
Nurses help people who are sick.		
The doctor thought his patient was the strongest person he had ever seen.		
The report said it was probably the worst storm in years.		
In Cuba, people speak Spanish.		
The Jamaica Constabulary Force have their own band.		
Everyone who hears the band play is amazed by their music.		

What's your view?
Do you think facts or opinions are more important? Share your ideas with your friends.

Chapter 29

Grammar builder

Remember ☆☆☆

An **exclamation mark** can be used at the end of a sentence to show emotion.

Sentences with an exclamation mark can be funny, exciting, amazing, incredible, angry or sad.

1. Here are two sentences. The first is an exclamation and the second is not. Read the sentences to a partner. Remember, an exclamation is often something exciting, funny, unusual, joyful or amazing, so you should sound that way, too.
   - *The athlete ran so fast that he broke the world record!*
   - *The athlete ran in a race against others from around the world.*

2. With your partner, discuss the two sentences. Why do you think the first sentence has an exclamation mark but the second does not? Share your ideas.

3. Here are some more sentences.

   Decide which punctuation mark to put at the end of each one.

   Choose from:

   1. Have you eaten the mango_____

   2. There are 28 island nations in the Caribbean_____

   3. Julie was so happy that she jumped for joy_____

   4. How long will hurricane watch last for_____

   5. I have never seen anything so beautiful_____

Look and learn

Conjunctions are words that join different parts of a sentence together. Common conjunctions include the following: *and, but, or, so*. Below are examples of the conjunction *but*.

We can use the word *but* when we want to talk about **differences**.

For example: *In Jamaica people speak English, but in Haiti people speak French.*

Notice a comma is used before the word *but*.

4 Match the sentence halves. The first one is done for you.

1. In Haiti, people speak French,
2. Bananas are tasty,
3. The flag of Jamaica is green and yellow,
4. Cream is used in cooking,

a. but mangoes are tastier.
b. but in Cuba, people speak Spanish.
c. but coconut milk is used more often.
d. but the flag of Cuba is red, white and blue.

5 Now, write three sentences of your own using the word *but*. Make sure to include capital letters, full stops and the comma before the word *but*.

1. _____
2. _____
3. _____

Chapter 29

Let's write

1. Choose an island in the Caribbean other than Jamaica. Find a book to read about this island. It could be a book about sports, a famous person or food from that country, or it could be about well-known places there.

2. Read the book. Then complete the book report.
   - Describe the book. For example: *This book is about Trinidad and Tobago. It describes the islands' history. It also…*
   - Colour the stars to give the book a rating.
   - Explain why you enjoyed or didn't enjoy the book.

   For example: *I enjoyed the book because it was interesting / exciting / funny to read.*

   I didn't enjoy the book because it was boring. I don't like books about history.

Book title: _____

Author: _____

Describe what your book is about:

Rate your book:
5 Best book I've ever read.
4 Great book.
3 Good book.
2 It was OK.
1 I didn't enjoy it.

☆ ☆ ☆ ☆ ☆

Explain why you enjoyed it or did not enjoy it:

311

Term 3 Unit 1

Chapter 30

Speaking and listening

> **Look and learn**
>
> The **present continuous** is used to talk about something that is happening at the time of speaking. The action is not finished. For example: *He **is** paint**ing** the wall.*

1. With your partner, look around the classroom and take turns to describe activities that you can see. Think about the nouns in the classroom and how they are being used. For example: *Anna is sitting at her desk* or *Dylon is colouring with his crayons.*

2. Point to things you can see in the picture and discuss them with a partner. What is happening? For example: *A boy is walking a dog on a lead.*

The Grand Hotel

Chapter 30

Look and learn

- Generally, we use *will* + a main verb to talk about the future. For example:

  What will you do tomorrow?
  *I **will go** to school.*

- We often use *will be*. For example:

  What will you look like in five years' time?
  *I **will be** much taller.*

3 In small groups, imagine a photograph is taken of the Grand Hotel in the same place in five years' time. What do you think will be different? Discuss your ideas with your group. Think about the walls, the windows, the ground, the people, plants and trees, etc.

Example:
I am sure there **will be** a lot of trees around the buildings.

ICT opportunity

Many zoos around the world have set up cameras so you can watch the animals at any time. With an adult's help, find a live camera at a zoo. Describe what the animals are doing in the **present continuous** tense.

Word builder

The letter *x* makes different sounds in different words. These words all contain the letter *x*.

Word box

x-ray	exit	xylophone	sixty
exam	fox	taxi	fix
luxury	box	mixing	wax

Look and learn

- Sometimes the letter *x* sounds like *ks*: *box*.
- Sometimes the letter *x* sounds like *gz*: *exam*.
- Sometimes the letter *x* sounds like *eks*: *x-ray*.
- Sometimes the letter *x* sounds like *z*: *xylophone*.
- Sometimes the letter *x* sounds like *gz*: *luxury*.

1   Read the words to a partner. Pay attention to the sound of the letter *x*. What type of *x* sound does each word have?

2   Write the word from the word box to match each description.

   1   a number greater than 59: _____

   2   a musical instrument: _____

   3   a type of transport: _____

4 the way out: _____

5 material that candles are made from: _____

6 a test: _____

Remember ☆☆☆

Letters in a word that we do not say are called **silent letters**.

3 Say the words to a partner. Together, decide which letter is the silent letter

	Silent letter
wrap	
thumb	
castle	
walk	
knob	
guess	
school	
answer	

Let's read

1 Read the article and answer the questions.

Grand Hotel opening soon

The Grand Hotel opens next week. It will be the tallest hotel with 30 floors in total. Guests will have to use an elevator to get to the restaurant the top floor.

There will be 500 luxury bedrooms. Bedrooms will have all modern technology including super-fast Wi-Fi and USB charge points for cell phones. Three hundred of the bedrooms will have a bathroom with a bubbly jacuzzi bath.

The Skyview restaurant will be run by top chef Vincente Nistaze who has come from Italy. The hotel owner believes people will want to come to the hotel just to taste Vincente's cooking. In his words, "Vincente's food is some of the best in the world".

Head Chef Vincente Nistaze

The hotel will have a rooftop swimming pool as well as an indoor pool, gym and spa. In the hotel grounds there are two full-size tennis courts and beautiful gardens. There is also a children's adventure playground with swings and play equipment.

1. What is the heading of the article?

   _____

2. What job does the man in the photograph do?

   _____

3. Fill in the missing information. Use facts from the article. You do not need to write in complete sentences.

Number of floors:	
Total number of bedrooms:	
Number of bathrooms with a jacuzzi:	
Name of head chef:	
Number of swimming pools:	
Other sports you can do:	
Things for children to use:	

4. What is the hotel owner's opinion about Vincente's cooking? Tick (✓) the box.

   He thinks it is great. ☐   He thinks it is terrible. ☐

5. Would you like to stay at this hotel? Talk to a partner. Say why you would, or wouldn't like to stay there.

Grammar builder

Look and learn

- We use an **apostrophe** (*'s* or *s'*) to show that something belongs to **one** person or thing. For example: *Winston's car*; *Ross' bag*. (The apostrophe must come at the end of the name if it already ends in *s*).

- We use an apostrophe after the *s* (*s'*) at the end of a **plural** noun to show possession. For example: *Here are the **girls'** bags. This is my **parents'** car.*

- When **plural** nouns do not end in *s*, for example, *children, men, women*, we use an apostrophe *s* (*'s*). For example: **children's** *classroom*, **men's** *toilet*, **women's** *changing room*.

1 Complete the sentences. Use the apostrophe in the correct way to show possession in each sentence. Be careful, some words already end in *s*!

1 Where is _____ mixing bowl? (Grandma)

2 _____ taxi is coming at 8 o'clock. (Jordan)

3 It's the _____ box. (girls)

4 They are all the _____ toys. (dogs)

5 Look on the _____ table for the pencils. (children)

Remember ☆ ☆ ☆

There are three main tenses: the **past**, the **present** and the **future**.

To talk about the future, we use *will* before verbs.

For example: *I will be.*

Talking about the future

2 Read the article about the Grand Hotel in the "Let's read" lesson again. Use a ruler to underline examples of sentences with the future tense using *will*.

3 Look at the picture in the "Speaking and listening" lesson again. Remember talking about what the Grand Hotel will be like in five years' time? Write two sentences to say what you think it will be like. For example: *I think the buildings will be taller.*

_____

_____

Term 3 Unit 1

Let's write

L👀k and learn

We use the word *not* to make a sentence negative.

For example: *A banana is yellow.* (positive); *A banana is **not** pink.* (negative)

We can shorten *not* and combine it with verbs.

For example: *have not* becomes *haven't*, and *do not* becomes *don't*.

- *I haven't got a pen.*
- *I don't want to play.*

1 Tick (✓) the items that are not yellow.

320

2 Complete the sentences using *have to* or *don't have to*.

1. You _____ brush your teeth every day.

2. Guests _____ use the elevator to reach the restaurant on the top floor.

3. Children _____ go to school every day of the week.

4. We _____ drink water to stay healthy.

5. Children _____ listen closely in class.

6. Some children _____ wear uniform for school.

3 Imagine that you went to the market with a list. You ticked off the items you bought.

Write sentences to say what you <u>do not</u> have. There are three things, so you need to write three sentences. For example:
I *have not got mangoes. I haven't got a pineapple.*

1. _____

2. _____

3. _____

yams ✓
bananas ✓
rice ✗
peas ✓
tomatoes ✓
chicken ✗
peppers ✗

Term 3 Unit 1 Review and assessment

Speaking and listening

1. The Caribbean people are similar in many ways, but there are also some differences. In pairs, talk about what they share in common and their differences. Think about language, food, music, etc.

Word builder

1. Write "L" for living things or "NL" for non-living things. There are six words in each group.

   spider _____   tree   _____

   river   _____   frog   _____

   ball   _____   fish   _____

   plant   _____   dominoes _____

   thunder _____   fire   _____

   car   _____   grass   _____

2. Write "fiction" or "non-fiction".

Writing about things that are true or that happened.	
Writing about things that are not true.	

Review and assessment

3 Write "F" for fiction or "NF" for non-fiction.

1 A book about the history of Jamaica. _____

2 A book of Anansi stories. _____

3 A book of recipes to cook at home. _____

4 A book about maths. _____

5 A book of *Aesop's fables*. _____

Read the paragraph about teeth and answer the following questions.

> You use your teeth to chew food. Babies are born without teeth; they cannot chew food. Teeth start to grow through the gums when a baby is about six months old. As the baby grows, more teeth come through until eventually there are 20 teeth. Children have ten teeth on the bottom and ten teeth on the top. These teeth are sometimes called *milk teeth*. When a child is about nine or ten, some of the milk teeth can start to feel loose. This is because adult teeth are starting to push through. Milk teeth fall out naturally and are replaced by adult teeth. There are more adult teeth than milk teeth; an adult has 32 teeth in total. You can look after your teeth by brushing them twice a day with toothpaste and by visiting the dentist.

1 Read and tick (✓) the correct answer.

1 Why can't babies chew food?

   Babies only like milk. ☐

   Babies don't like food. ☐

   Babies don't have teeth. ☐

2 Children's teeth become loose when they are about seven years old.

   true ☐   false ☐

3 How many times a day should you brush your teeth?

   one ☐   two ☐   three ☐

4 Who can help us take care of our teeth?

   paramedic ☐   doctor ☐   dentist ☐

5 Which of these sentences is an opinion?

   Babies grow more teeth as they get older. ☐

   Adults have more teeth than children ☐

   Brushing your teeth is more important than going to the dentist. ☐

Review and assessment

Grammar builder

1 The flag of Haiti has two colours; blue on the top half and red on the bottom half.

  1 Which word from the sentence is a proper noun? Circle.
     flag   Haiti   blue

  2 Which word from the sentence is an adjective? Circle.
     flag   Haiti   blue

2 A *plural* is when there is more than one of something. What is the plural of each of these words? The first one is done for you.

girl → ___girls___   child → _____

hotel → _____   man → _____

boy → _____   prize → _____

country → _____   nurse → _____

lady → _____   bay → _____

Let's write

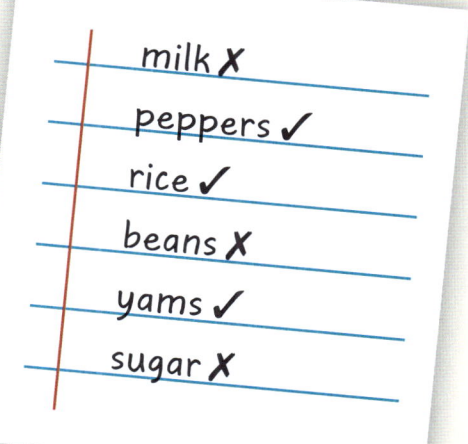

1 Imagine that you went to the shop with a list. You ticked off the items you bought.

Write sentences to say what you <u>do not</u> have. There are three things, so you need to write three sentences. For example:
I haven't got a pineapple.

1 _____

2 _____

3 _____

325